Finding
your way
in Asheville
(fourth edition)
(yikes!)
(already?)

by Cecil Bothwell

Brave Ulysses Books
2011

Finding your way in Asheville
Fourth edition
ISBN-13:978-1456379896
Copyright 2005, 2009, 2011
Cecil Bothwell
All rights reserved
Brave Ulysses Books
POB 1877
Asheville, NC 28802
braveulysses.com
cover photos by Cecil Bothwell
Front-Lexington Gateway Mural:Asheville Mural Project
Back-Simple Gift: Sally Bryenton, and
Seated Woman: Ben Betsalel (pictured before it was defaced)

also by the author

•*Whale Falls: An exploration of belief and its consequences*
2010
•*The Prince of War: Billy Graham's Crusade for a Wholly Christian Empire*
2007/2010
•*Can we have archaic and idiot?*
2009
•*Pure Bunkum: Reporting on the life and crimes of Buncombe County Sheriff Bobby Lee Medford*
2008
•*Garden My Heart: Organic Strategies for Backyard Sustainability*
2008
•*The Icarus Glitch: Another Duck Soup Reader*
2002
•*Gorillas in the Myth: A Duck Soup Reader*
2001 & 2008 (second edition)

Finding your way in Asheville 2011/2012

PLEASE NOTE: Although I have more or less done my best to ensure that all of the information herein is accurate as this fourth (yikes!) edition goes to press, change happens. I once made a mistake (though I am fast approaching perfection). Phone ahead before you make BIG plans. I can assume no liability for spoiled days, grumpy moods or other miasma caused by your failure to plan ahead. Opinions expressed are those of the several authors (mostly mine) and may or may not be well reasoned or incisive. But they're ours and we like them. Stores, restaurants, clubs and historic persons mentioned herein should be inordinately pleased to show up on our radar at all, and griping is a sure way to avoid inclusion in subsequent editions. Unlike many city and tourist guides, I/we have accepted no payment and solicited no advertising dollars in regard to this volume.

Also, I haven't listed any places to stay. I figured most of you have already arrived and figured that part out, or researched it elsewhere. Everybody has a different perspective on comfort and affordability. Besides, I wanted to keep this thing small enough to fit in a purse or glove compartment. There are tons of wonderful B&Bs in this city and lots of info online.

Warning! Warning! Warning!

If your idea of a great vacation is shopping at a mall (or, shudder, an *outlet* mall) and eating at national chain restaurants, you have just wasted your money on this book. Now would be a good time to return to the independent bookseller where you bought it and politely ask for a refund. Yes, Virginia, Asheville has a mall and a lot of chain restaurants and if you need a guide book to find them you are in a kind of trouble that we are not qualified to address.

Look under "Counselors" in the Yellow Pages.

I am not going to direct you to national chain anything. I have mentioned tiny regional chains if I decided they are unique enough to warrant it. (I have mentioned a couple of megalithic national chain somethings, but only to facilitate driving directions to really wonderful places. Ah, the vicissitudes of authorship!)

Welcome to Asheville! Or, if you are an old timer, welcome to this book. Either way, I'm glad you're here and want to help you figure out the best way to spend whatever part of your life you have decided to spend in these mountains.

How to use this book:

This guide is based on the way real people really visit a city, or at least the way I think real people should really visit a city. Going to eight different places in distal parts of town in one day not only wastes nonrenewable resources and generates air pollution, it fritters your valuable tourist time. There is more to life than driving and parking.

Walking, particularly in a city of Asheville's walkable scale, generates memories of gargoyles and trees and flowers and bricks and faces and sounds and smells. Real stuff. Driving generates memories of your dashboard and your windshield and your rear-view mirror and that irritating grinding metallic noise somewhere under the hood that you are praying isn't going to be as expensive as it sounds.

Table of contents: page 11. <u>Index in the rear.</u>

Every **place, destination, shop** or **venue** I recommend is **bolded** upon first mention in any section, is included in the index—and is likely to be found in topical alphabetical listings.

In a **hurry?** Start on page 11, with

"Why am I here?"

What this book IS:

... A **SELECTIVE** guide to stuff even locals haven't necessarily discovered. A trip-tick to places and experiences that will stay glued to your mental sun-visor for years. A compendium of suggestions that will keep you entertained for a weekend or create a nodal point in your existence. The change could be permanent.

This little book is a hot date on a cold night and a cool breeze at 10 p.m. in August. Throw in a tasty cocktail and a little umbrella and live jazz oozing around the corner.

I aim to take you by the hand and lead you around as if you were a dear friend I wanted to mightily impress with what an incredible place I've decided to inhabit. In the course of this touring, I'll drop names of special places to eat, to drink, to gawk and walk, and on and on. While I'm rattling on about the good stuff I'm not going to get bogged down in details. I figure you are grown up enough to use the listings or you wouldn't be out touring on your own in the first place.

There are suggestions about where to take a hike or canoe, but I'll add some thoughts about how to come home in one piece and without an annoying rash.

You'll discover some unflattering truths about this town and its local heroes. If you prefer your heroes with pomade and lip gloss instead of warts and all, you will have to go to the Chamber of Commerce.

You'll find neighborhood visits and walks or tours, plus transportation and parking tips. But there are also directories (by category). Using them together you can fill out a day without driving around in circles asking directions and looking for new parking places between each stop. Note that most music venue shows don't start until 9 or even 11 p.m., so it makes some sense not to schedule club hopping for earlier in the day.

And, I've included some longer articles originally published elsewhere which illuminate some of the history and folklore of this lovely mountain town

What this book IS NOT:

This is **NOT A COMPREHENSIVE** guide to everything you have always heard about Asheville, particularly if you heard it on TV or read about it in a Sunday supplement or in-flight magazine.
Been there.
Done that.   Oh, sigh.

The usual suspects are only mentioned in passing—however glorious they may be: Great Smoky Mountains National Park, Biltmore Estate, Grove Park Inn ... you know the drill. There are metric tons of info about over-hyped tourist meccas available elsewhere. If they filled the hole in your traveler's soul you wouldn't have picked up this book in the first place. Right?
Nuff said.

Discouraging words:

You will probably like Asheville so much that you want to move here, and chances are you'll find yourself welcome. But ... be warned:

There is a lot of truth to the old saw about the necessity of bringing a job with you. Wages are low and housing costs are high (based on state averages). Sure we have a lot of restaurants, and the upside is that there are lots of folks who can afford to eat out. Huzzah!

But the bottom of the griddle is that we have **LOTS** of people willing to work in the service industry, who are happy to have any job at all. And no, we don't want you to build a new big box store here. Leave the mountains alone. If this place looked like where you came from, you wouldn't have spent a lot of money to get here in the first place.

Asheville anecdote—a true story!

Q: What do you do?
A: I'm on waitstaff at a little bistro.
Q: Where'd you get your MFA?

How this book is arranged

The authors and publisher have gone to extraordinary lengths to make this little book accessible to people, even people like you. (Yes, you.) Hence the previous page of helpful guidance, the following pages of congenial therapy helping you figure out why you are here in the first place, and the index at the back that pretty well covers the whole deal. You'll find maps of special sections of town as well.

This page sort of takes you by the hand and points you in the right direction. Aren't we wonderful people?

.

After you leave this front matter you will find:

Parking info: This section alone will easily pay for the book. (p. 13)

Maps and Neighborhoods: (the downtown divvied up into sections by street). This part should help you navigate geographically and includes descriptions of local shops and icons.

Walks and Gawks: How to see the real Asheville, on foot.

Family Fun: What to do with a crowd, particularly munchkins, sprouts or rug-gerbils.

Galleries, Food, Drink, Music: We got 'em!

Nature and the Great Outdoors: Because that is a big part of why we are here, we felt compelled to share.

The Giant Crystal Under the City: the low-down on the multifaceted and mysterious high point.

Historic glimpses: How this place ended up being Asheville.

Weather info: (bring a paddle and a canteen)

INDEX to *EVERYTHING ASHEVILLISH* p. 150

Why am I here? (Table of Contents)

The first question you need to answer is "Why am I here?" Not in any grand metaphysical sense, though that isn't a bad thing to think about while you walk around Asheville (see section on the Giant Crystal Under The City), but in the narrowest sense.

Why are you visiting Asheville today?

Mostly for the food? The music? The art? The local beer?

The architecture? The history? The scene? The scenery?

The sports?

The Federal Court System? (Admit nothing.)

The hospitals? (This too shall pass.)

The shopping?

The dead writers? (got lots)

Are you alone or with a lover or with all of your in-laws, outlaws and sundry kin?

Does your staff think you are hiking the Appalachian Trail? Is your companion Argentinian?

Why are you here, anyway?

- **Antiques?** (p.78)
- **Architecture?**
  - Check out the walk (p. 36)
- **Arts and crafts?** (Not to be confused with "Arts and Crafts")
    - Gallery Gawks (p. 55)
    - River Arts District (p. 60)
- **Asheville's Afro-History** (p. 141)
- **Bed and Breakfast?** (p. 6)
- **Beer?** (the local sort, p. 74)
    - Pub prowl (p. 75)

- **Books and Literary matters?**
    - Booksellers (p. 91)
    - Local authors (p. 88)
- **Brunch or Breakfast?** (p. 73)
- **Coffee shops?**
    - Lazy morning coffee/boutique stroll(p. 32)
    - Coffee/tea/bistro listings (p. 34)
- **Family?**
    - Family outings, (p. 42)
- **Festivals?**
    - Let us entertain you, for free! (p. 48)
- **Food?**
    - Restaurant listings on (p. 62)
- **Giant Crystal Under the City?** (pp. 10, 11, 12, 22, 83, 152)
- **GLBT?**
    - Out in Asheville (p. 86)
- **Hiking/Outdoor Sports?** (p. 93)
- **History?**
    - Check out Walks and Tours (p. 35, etc.)
    - Check out fascinating stories (start on p. 116)
- **Ice Cream or Dessert?** (p. 74)
- **Music?**
    - Forever on the verge (p. 79)
- **Nature**
    - See big nature section starting p. 98
- **Shopping?**
    - Check out neighborhoods (p. 17)
    - Check out the walks (p. 35)
- **Sports?**
    - High country low-down (p. 93)
    - Outfitter listings (p. 94)
    - See big nature section starting on p. 98
- **Tattoo?**
    - See where to get needled on p. 78
- **Theater?** (p. 87)

Downtown Parking

There's a lot of hype about a purported lack of parking in Asheville. Don't believe it. Yes, you may have to walk a block or two now and again. Mostly not. Here's the scoop on downtown parking.

Metered Spaces

Parallel and diagonal spaces are sprinkled throughout the city.

Meters run 8 a.m. - 6 p.m. Monday through Saturday. This means there's **FREE PARKING after 6 p.m. and all day and night on Sundays**. (As of this writing the city is considering extension of meter hours to **8 p.m.** - read the meter while you feed it!) Maximum time on most city meters is two hours and the city only charges $1.00/ hour. Cheap by national standards. This is patrolled pretty diligently during the day.

There is a metered 24/7 **private** parking lot on Page Ave., **under 24 hour guard.** You will be ticketed if you overstay.

City Parking Lots

The first hour in all <u>city</u> parking decks is free.

• **Civic Center Deck** (access on Haywood St. and Rankin Ave.)
Monday through Friday 10 a.m. - 7 p.m.
First hour- free, then .50/hour
$4 max. /$1 flat fee after 7 p.m. and on Saturday and Sunday.
• **Rankin Avenue Deck** (access on Rankin and Walnut)
Monday through Friday 10 a.m.- 7 p.m.
First hour- free, then .50/hour
$4 max./$1 flat fee after 7 p.m. and on weekends.

Wall Street Parking Deck (access on corner of Otis St. and Wall St.)
Monday through Friday 10 a.m. - 7 p.m.
First hour- free, .75/hour
$6 max./$2 flat fee after 7:00 p.m. and on weekends.

Buncombe County Parking Deck (access on College St., across from Buncombe County Courthouse) No free time. Ever.
24/7, $1 per hour, $8 max for 24 hours.

Private Parking Lots

Walnut Street Lot (access on Walnut Street across from Mellow Mushroom)
$2 first hour, $1 each additional hour, $5 max.

Haywood Park Hotel (access on Battery Park) Metered spaces
24-hours - .75/hour

Biltmore Avenue: (near Pack Place)
.50/ first half hour
$2 first hour/$1 every hour after, $8 max.
$3.00 flat fee after 4 p.m. and Saturday and Sunday

Corner of Biltmore and Aston (access on Aston St., across from Barley's Taproom)
$1 hour Monday-Saturday/$2 flat fee after 6 p.m. and Sunday

40 South Lexington (access on Lexington Ave., corner of Aston and Lexington)
No parking during weekday/$2 flat fee after 6 p.m. and weekends

There's **FREE** parking all along **Cherry Street** if you don't mind a walk. Please take **Flint Street Bridge** (crosses I-240) to walk on into town. As a rule, towing is enforced in Asheville—please read the signs carefully. You may find yourself buying your car back for 150 bucks.

you are here **X**

Transportation, Maps, and Neighborhoods

On the following pages I've drawn little maps of small sections of town that ought to help you navigate on foot. You will find a number of free, city-wide maps in racks and on counters all around town and I suggest you avail yourself of one.

Orientation

Vance Monument, located in **Pack Square**, is a useful centering landmark even if the traffic pattern there is somewhat baffling.

The major east-west streets through town are **College Street** and **Patton Avenue**. College runs from the Beaucatcher Tunnel on the east side and merges with Patton in **Pritchard Park**. Patton stretches from Vance Monument, west across the French Broad River to **West Asheville**. Downtown, for several blocks, College is one way west-bound and Patton is one way east-bound (downtown).

The major north-south route is **Merrimon Avenue/Broadway/Biltmore Avenue**, which is all one road but given multiple names in order to keep people confused and prevent creation of a popular, democratic society with universal health care, social justice, no war and free beer. This street intersects with Patton at the Vance Monument.

Interstate 240 runs generally east-west through the city, connecting to I-40 on each end of town. **Interstate 40** runs east-west on the south side of town. **Interstate 26** is theoretically an east-west highway, but runs sort of north-south through Asheville with a west-east hook. The Interstate maze around and through the city was designed by hung-over DOT planners on the morning after an unusually raucous New Year's party. If it doesn't thoroughly confuse you, you aren't paying attention.

• The **Asheville-Hendersonville Regional Airport** is south of town— you get there by taking I-26 East (which, as noted, actually takes you west by south).
• The **Blue Ridge Parkway** runs from northeast to southwest along the east and south edges of the city.
• **Great Smoky Mountains National Park** is west of Asheville (take I-40 W, or the Parkway if you're in no hurry).
• The bus depot is on the east end of Beaucatcher Tunnel (follow College Street east from downtown) and the nearest passenger rail service is in Greenville, South Carolina (we're working on this).

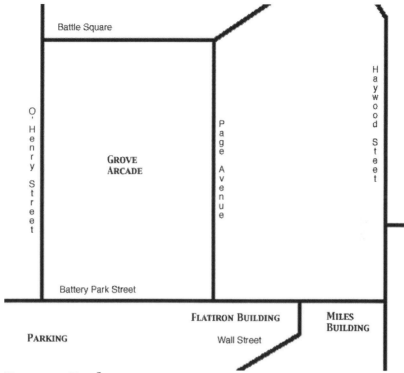

Battery Park [top of map is North]

What was once Battery Park Hill is now a low rise in Asheville's downtown—the hill was carted away to fill a ravine (now Coxe Avenue).

The centerpiece of this section of the city is the magnificent **Grove Arcade**, an unfinished monument to a patent medicine salesman's unquestionable self-aggrandizement and questionable tonic. Originally constructed as an open-air market and base for a 20-story tower, the grandiose scheme was halted by Grove's death and the Depression. Later the Federal Government purchased the building, boarded up its open air stalls and painted everything grey.

Finally the city reclaimed the building from the Feds and leased it to Carolina Power and Light (now Progress Energy) for $1 per year. With the building itself untaxed, and aided by substantial tax incentives for historical renovation, CP&L managed to scrape together enough cash to fix up the joint. It was reopened as a retail, office and apartment complex in the Fall of 2003 with a stated goal of fostering local businesses relevant to local people. Now it's pretty much aimed at tourists.

The Arcade is currently home to a diversity of shops and galleries, though several of the first entries barely lasted a year.

Survivors include the ever-helpful and friendly **Grove Arcade Copy Shop**, **Kamm's Kustard**, **Mountain Made** (crafts), **Enter the Earth** (geological marvels), and **Mission at the Grove** (Arts and Crafts reproductions).

Newcomers in the past year or so include: **Battery Park Champagne Bar, Carolina Cigar Company**, **Roberto Coin**, and **Stevenson's Rare Coins & Jewelry**. Restaurants include **Carmels' Restaurant and Bar**, **Cats and Dawgs**, **Chorizo** (Latin)**, Modesto** (pizza), **True Confections**, **Santé** wine bar, **The Eye Center**, **Thai Basil**. Other businesses are moving in all the time and some are bound to survive.

RENCI at UNC Asheville has occupied part of the building, and has a dual focus: 1) on disaster research, mitigation, and preparedness, taking advantage of Western North Carolina's expertise in weather and climate modeling, visualization, and public outreach, and 2) spurring local economic development.

On the north end the Arcade faces the towering Battery Park Apartments—once upon a time a hotel. The present structure replaced a previous Battery Park Hotel from whose top floor suite George Vanderbilt watched progress on his mansion in what is now Biltmore. The right wing of the building offer food and beverage and smokes. **Havana** delivers great Cuban food, with a full bar. A cigar store, **Bonnie's Little Corner**, occupies a small space in the venue.

Page Avenue runs along the east side of the Arcade. There's a **Kimmel Trading** (art) and **Airsoft Games** (electronic and others), and at the north end you'll find the **Captain's Bookshelf** (see Literary Matters, p. 89), a marvelous collection of rare, unusual, obscure and fascinating books.

If you continue up Page between Captain's and the Battery Park Apartments you will confront **Basilica St. Lawrence** (see Architectural Walk, p. 36) and the **Asheville Civic Center**. A right turn puts you on Haywood Street.

At its south end the Arcade fronts on Battery Park Avenue. On the far side of the street to the left of the parking deck, there is a row of shops in the **Flatiron Building** (see Architectural Walk, p. 36).

Street Fair may have the largest collection of earrings in the Western Hemisphere in addition to eclectic clothing and accessories.

Heading east you'll find boutiques including **Va-Va-Voom**, **Bella's**, **Natural Selections**, **Blaze n Skyy** (dogs), **Feathers & Needlepoint**, followed by **Kilwin's Chocolate Fudge and Ice Cream** (what's a shopping jaunt without chocolate?). After dessert you can stop for lunch at **Chai Pani** (Indian) or a beverage and more dessert at **World Coffee**.

Across the street, in the ground floor of an architecturally challenged condominium high-rise at 21 Battery Park, step into the **Three Dog Bakery** to discover a world of treats and gear for your favorite pup.

Cross back to **A Far Away Place** which fronts on both Battery Park and Wall Street with its marvelous offering of stuff from ... you guessed it, far away places! (Hey, you catch on quick!) When you reach the large sculpture of an iron, intended to celebrate the Flatiron Building but confusingly situated adjacent to the Miles Building (which is therefore constantly confused with the Flatiron – people somehow missing the point that the Flatiron Building has the footprint of, yes, a flat iron) (whew) you are at the intersection with **Wall Street**.

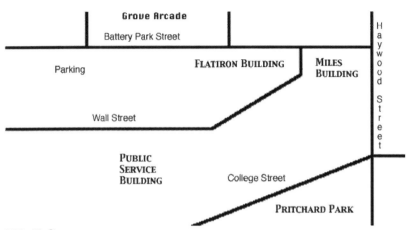

Wall Street [top of map is North]

Wall Street boasts a diverse collection of shops and restaurants including one of the best breakfast- and certainly the best lunch-spot in town, **Early Girl Eatery** and, what many used to argue offered Asheville's premier dining experience, **The Market Place (new owner, jury out).** Down the way you will find **Cucina 24 Restaurant and Bar**, and **The Laughing Seed Restaurant**, grande dame of Asheville's vegetarian food purveyors with **Jack of the Wood** brew pub downstairs (fronting on Patton Avenue). **Wall St. Coffee House** and **Bake it Pretty** round out the food court.

Consumer goods include handmade sandals at **Paul Taylor Custom Sandals & Belts**, stuff from far away places at **A Far Away Place**, **Celtic Way** (clothing), **Spellbound Books** (chilren's reading haven). **Fired Up!** (do-it-yourself ceramic art, with walk-ins welcome), **Purl's Yarn Emporium**, and half of all the beads you will ever need at **Beads & Beyond**. Jewelers include **Overstrøm Studio Fine Art Jewelry** and **Wicke & Greene Estate Jewelry**.

The other tall building on Wall Street is the **Public Service Building (renamed Self Help)**— once owned by the big gas company, but now owned by **Public Interest Projects** (see Daddy's Money, p. 114).

Wall Street is home to the **Jubilee! Community**, an eclectic church open to all, whose pastor and founder, Howard Hanger combines Judeo-Christianity with infusions from every other spiritual tradition, music, dance, theater and humor to create what can only be described as a world religion.

Adjacent to Jubilee! you can get a good look at the wall for which Wall Street is named (lean over the railing and look for the pair of bronze rats — part of the **Urban Trail**).

This is a good place to get some sense of the topography of oldtimey Asheville. Looking out beyond the parking lot below you, you can see Asheland Avenue falling away toward the south. The wall beneath your feet was built to permit development of Battery Park Hill whose peak was once approximately where the Grove Arcade sits today (behind you as you face the railing).

Across Wall Street from Jubilee!, next to Climbax, a stairway takes you up to Battery Park Ave.

Secret passage: There is a doorway right beside Paul Taylor sandals that leads to a stairway that dumps you out in Pritchard Park.

If you continue to the end of Wall Street you'll dead-end into Otis Street. A right turn takes you back to Battery Park Avenue, a left, to Patton Avenue. You will also see a large iron sculpture next to the Federal Courthouse. It certainly is rusty, isn't it?

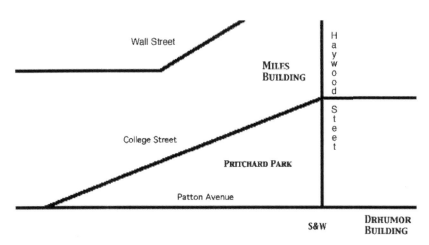

Pritchard Park [top of map is North]

This is the heart of Asheville, or at least the source of its heartbeat. Many Friday nights in clement weather a drum circle gathers in the amphitheater of Pritchard Park to regulate the pulse of the city. Bounded by Haywood Street, College Street and Patton Avenue, this is where Asheville comes together. **The Giant Crystal Under the City** may well be located directly below the hot dog cart on the north side of this park, adjacent to **Spiritex**, which sells local and organic clothing.

Corner House, **Jerusalem Garden**, **Kathmandu**, **Mayfel's**, **Steak & Wine** and **Tupelo Honey** offer food, with **Loretta's** lunches just up the block on Patton and the best traditional breakfast in Asheville at the **Mediterranean Restaurant** up the other block on College. Meanwhile, **Asheville Yacht Club**, **Jack of the Wood,** the **College Street Pub, Satchel's Bar, Thirsty Monk**, and **Weinhaus** provide drinks. Walk around to the back of the "purple building" to find **Firestorm Cafe and Books** for healthy jolt of progressive politics with your coffee or tea.

For visual splendor visit **A Boy and His Dog, Aesthetic Gallery**, the **Asheville Gallery of Art** and **10,000 Villages**, a craft store selling the work of third world artisans who are paid a fair price for their work— a craft store with a social conscience.

Secret Passage! *There's a secret passage to Wall Street, through the door under the clock.*

If you need over-the-counter medication, prescriptive drugs, film or breath fresheners, don't miss **Asheville Discount Pharmacy**, a locally owned drug store on the south side of the park.

North Lexington Avenue and Broadway

Woodfin Street

N. Lexington Ave.

Carolina Lane

Broadway

Walnut Street

College Street

[top of map is North]

Lexington Avenue is the precise epicenter of Asheville's edgiest art and social experimentation and is therefore the district most threatened by development.

North Lex runs north from College Street toward I-240. Starting from College, on the west side is **Tops for Shoes**, which has maintained its "foothold" since 1952. Tops wraps around Adorn Salon, a very popular styling outfit which fronts on College.

Across from Tops you'll find **Atelier** gallery, the **Chevron Trading Post and Bead Company**, **Mountain Lights** (candles and more), **Funky Mutt**, **Write On** (stationery, natch), **Cosmic Vision**, and **Instant Karma** (a counter-cultural emporium with smoke supplies). The **Costume Shoppe** is there too, to make you look like someone else.

Crossing Walnut (still headed downhill on the east side of the street) find **Cornerstone Minerals** (a rock shop). On the opposite side the first shop is Terra Nostra (more earthy artifacts) and **Gaea— Gifts for the Soul. Nest Organics**, next in line, supplies bed clothes, linens and housewares, while **Spiritex Mia** delivers a wonderful array of organic clothing. North Lex seems to be the organic textile hub of Asheville these days.

Readers shouldn't pass up a chance to visit **Downtown Books and New**s, a singular source for used books and current periodicals, from the Grey Lady to eclectica.

On a Roll screen printing is downtown Asheville's primary source for politically charged tee-shirts and other hip printed matter. **Hip Replacements** at 72 North Lex has the best resale shop name ever with merchandise to suit and near-neighbor **Terra Diva** offers some glorious women's wear. **Virtue**, **Minx** and **Honeypot** round out the N. Lex clothiers. **Octopus Garden** is a smoke shop with counter-cultural accessories. **Liquid Dragon Tattoo** and **Forever Tattoo** ply the skin trade, and **Crucible Glass Works** is a studio/gallery offering North Lex restaurants/ bars: **Green Light Cafe** (vegan), **BoBo's** (gallery), **Bouchon** (French), **Mela** (Indian), **HeiwaShokudo** (Japanese), **Southern**, **Lex Ave. Brewing** (LAB). **Izzy's Coffee Den** has become the latest home for the coffee-loving refugees of the Lexington

Ave. arts crowd. It is also one of the few places in town that offer breakfast cereals on their regular menu. Next door is **Dobra Tea**.

Just before Lex ducks under the Interstate, **Rosetta's Kitchen** looms above the fray. Open early and very late, Rosetta's serves dependably excellent vegetarian and vegan fare in a setting

that resonates with the **real** Asheville. Near Rosetta's find the **Emerald Lounge**, **Nova** and **Broadways**—for happening music. Continue under I-240 and north a couple of blocks to find **The Dripolator**, #2 to Izzy's as Asehville's favorite coffeehouse.

Between Lex and Broadway, on Walnut is **Scully's**, an old-fashioned neighborhood bar with a great courtyard space open in clement weather.

The block between Lex and Broadway, framed by Walnut Street and Woodfin Street, is threaded by **Carolina Lane** and Chicken Alley. Here you will find some of Asheville's cuttingest, undergroundest art, performance and social experimentation. (See "Carolina Lane" on p. 59)

Broadway

Traveling north on Broadway from College, there are a series of eateries on your left starting with **Green Sage Coffeehouse** (which old-timers still remember as the site of Asheville's legendary coffee house, Beanstreets). Continuing north, newcomer **Suwana's**

Thai Orchid has already gained an enthusiastic following, that's followed by **Old Europe Coffee**, and **Wasabi** (sushi). A bit further on the left, find the legendary **Salsa**, **Tingle's Cafe** (resurection of a landmark restaurant, dating back to 1918) and **Sazerac**.

Shops in the first block include **Finkelstein's Loan**, Asheville's longest enduring pawn shop (1903). Across the street you'll find **Smoky's After Dark** (a self-identified gay bar) and **Tressa's Downtown** (jazz).

Looking up to your left as you cross Walnut Street you'll see the sign for the defunct Asheville Fish Company. further north on Broadway you find **Namasté Yoga**, the **Black Mountain College Museum**, and **Lost Objects Found Treasures** (L.O.F.T.) as well as **Bruisin' Ales**, with more than 700 brews (can you believe it?) and the recently opened **Olive or Twist** with big screen TVs on most walls and live jazz on many nights.

There are numerous antique dealers on both N. Lex and Broadway.

Two former downtown coffeehouses have moved slightly north. **Beans & Berries** (coffee and smoothies) has traveled north on Broadway where it becomes Merrimon a few blocks beyond I-240, and **The Dripolator**, mentioned above, is technically located on North Broadway (which is actually N. Lex after it ducks under I-240.) We have no intention of making this easy for you to follow. This is all part of keeping Asheville weird.

South Lexington Avenue

South Lex is nearly bereft of retail ventures but one rates special mention. The **French Broad Chocolate Lounge** at 2 South Lexington Avenue (just off Patton Ave.) is to die for. Chocolate drinks (including martinis), liquid truffles, baked goods, teas, coffees, candies, microbrews and more.

Biltmore Avenue

[top of map is North]

Asheville has at least its fair share of anomalous addresses—streets where the numbers abruptly reverse from "low-to high" to "high-to-low," for instance, or multiple streets with the same name.

But Merrimon/Broadway/Biltmore/ Hendersonville Road may be the most confusing to newcomers, principally because it is a major artery.

Biltmore Avenue begins at the Vance Monument and runs south to Biltmore. North of the Monument it is called **Broadway**. North of I-240 it is **Merrimon Avenue**. South of the town of Biltmore it's **Hendersonville Road**. Go figure.

If Pritchard Park constitutes the heart of Asheville, Pack Square comprises its head and stomach. From the west side of the intersection of Patton Avenue, Broadway and Biltmore a cluster of restaurants beckons the hungry wanderer. Facing the Vance Monument are the **Posana Cafe**, **Noodle Shop** and **Bistro 1896**. In the same block, **Kanpai Sushi Thai** and **Kubos Japanese Sushi** bracket **Jimmy John's Gourmet Sandwich** shop.

Turning your back on this restaurant row and looking past the monument, you'll see the mirrored glass of the Akzona Building, (designed by I.M. Pei on a bad day.) and rotating a 90 degrees clockwise, you'll be aimed at **The New French Bar** about halfway down the block on the other side of Biltmore. (there was never an old one, though the *old* New French Bar is now the **Flying Frog,** on Haywood St. which those of us who've been here a while think of as the "new" Frying Flog, which, by the way, does not flog fries.)

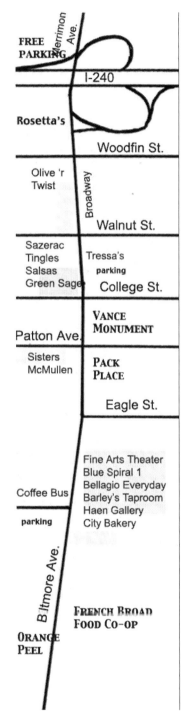

Beyond and behind the Akzona, and mentioned here only because there wasn't any other logical place to put them, sit the **Cottonwood Café**, at 122 College Street, and **Vincenzo's Ristorante & Bistro**, at 10 N. Market Street. (See restaurant listings, p. 62)

As you rotate your body, your eyes will sweep across **Pack Place**, an educational wonderland. This complex includes the **Asheville Art Museum** (in what was formerly Pack Library), the **Colburn Gem and Mineral Museum**, **Diana Wortham Theater** and the **Health Adventure**. If you had xray eyes, you could look through that complex and see the **YMI Cultural Center**, also part of the Pack Place ensemble, located in the next block at the corner of Eagle and Market Streets.

Back to food. In the next couple of blocks south on Biltmore you'll find the **Double Decker Coffee Bus**, **Laurey's Catering Service** (and restaurant), the **Asheville Wine Market** and **Mamacita's** on the west side of the street. **City Bakery, and the French Broad Food Co-op** (natural foods grocery open to non-members) are on the east. Just off Biltmore, on Eagle Street, find **Limones**, and **Ophelias.**

And returning from stomach to head: you'll find **Mast General Store**, **Indo Apparel and Gifts**, **Ariel Gallery,** Van Dyke Jewelry, and **Karmasonics**. Across the way, the **Fine Arts Theater** marquee stands out —a historic downtown movie house showing the best in current cinema. (Art, not blockbusters.)

Next door, and under the same ownership, is **Blue Spiral 1 Gallery**, the largest private gallery in the region, and *not* to be missed. Next door find **Bellagio Everyday** (art to wear). One block south **Haen Gallery** offers an ever-shifting montage of superb paintings and sculpture by modern masters.

West Asheville

Our Fair City has another downtown, fledgling to be sure, but with a storied past and a promising future. West Asheville, once-upon-a-time an independent city, is quickly becoming the community of choice for young families and new small businesses.

The reasons are many and include: an aging population of homeowners now moving on to retirement housing or cemeteries, thus freeing up housing stock; ditto for commercial property; rocketing prices downtown that make West 'ville a relative bargain; and, perhaps most important, a renewed sense of community. A few folks committed to a West Asheville renaissance became several and then a crowd. Now it's what's happening.

From a visitor's perspective, the core of West 'ville is Haywood Road, which describes a wide crescent through the neighborhood, and the linchpin is planted in the 700 block. It's there you'll find the **Westville Pub** and **West End Bakery**, the evening and morning hang-outs of choice for many Westvillians. The parking lot between these two mainstays is the scene of the local farmer's market and the back lot the setting for wildly popular monthly walk-in outdoor movies in the summer months. The **West Village Market & Cafe**, an urban grocery, shares a building with the Pub, and **Orbit DVD**. Across the street and a few doors west, don't miss **Digable Pizza**, which uses "as many organic and natural ingredients as possible" and uses them with panache, as well as the **Universal Joint**, a hip pub housed in an old Pure gas station.

A short walk southeast on Haywood brings you to **Beanwerks Coffee & Tea** (probably the second most politically progressive of the regions' coffee houses, after **Firestorm**) and **Tolliver's Crossing Irish Pub** Cross one more street and you'll find **The Hop**, a seasonal scoopateria (serving the best ice cream in the city, from Ultimate Ice Cream on the east side of town), and then **Freaks and Geeks Tattoo Sideshow** and **Burgermeister** with burgers from either beast or bean.

There are two murals worth noting in this stretch of road. One delicious depiction on side of the West End Bakery and the other three short blocks past The Hop at the corner of Jarrett and Haywood Road—a night time scene of Asheville's twinkling lights as seen from a nearby mountain overlook.

In the 600 block there's used clothing galore, from **Twice Round Recycled Clothing** at the corner of Louisiana and Haywood, to the **Littlest Birds** and the way-too-cool **Deluxe Retro** (just past the intersection with State Street). New clothing includes **Moelietha's Shoes** and **Minx**. **Pro Bikes** offers great gear and great advice. In between you can find drinks at **Pineapple Jack's**, and great food at the **Lucky Otter** (which somewhat improbably specializes in burritos. Otters? Burritos?) and the **Sunny Point Café and Bakery** (breakfast and lunch presented with a flair).

As you drop into the 500 block you'll find the **Tastee Diner**, an old-fashioned eatery that has held forth since the 1950s, and **Gallery 520-Broad Edge Studio** (art).

After you cross I-240 you're in the 400 block, home to **Second Gear** (used sports) a handful of galleries. **A Touch of Glass** displays stained glass in a marvelous building built in 1922 to house a fire department; located at 421 Haywood (they do very up-to-date window stuff, too). Across the street you'll find Second Gear (second-hand sports gear), **Westwood Galleries**, **Image 420** (screen-printing), and **Lucky Dog Studios**. If you have the time you can learn how to print with a letterpress and bind your own book at **Book Works**. Adjacent to A Touch of Glass, and around a slight corner find **Harvest Records** which deals in used vinyl and CDs.

Continue a couple of blocks to find **Izzy's Coffee Den** (west) and down around the sharp left curve discover Asheville's finest desserts at **Short Street Cakes**.

West Asheville is also home to a growing Latino population and is the most bilingual section of the city. Consequently there are numerous eateries and stores with a decidedly Hispanic flavor, including: **La Empanada** (794); **La Catrachita** (791); **Mercado Mexicano** (747); **Doloros Jose Mina Mexican Restaurant** (521); and the already mentioned Lucky Otter. (All addresses are on Haywood Road.) On Patton Ave., find **Nona Mia**, and **Azteca** (a grocery and bakery).

Outdoor Mural walk-about
(starting from the intersection of Broadway and Woodfin)

It's May, your company is holding a convention downtown and you've been cooped up inside for two of the three days. The Bradford pear trees have opened their delicate blooms and the redbuds are bursting. You promised yourself to visit some art galleries during the "free until 4 p.m." time block on your schedule. Decisions, decisions.

Do you really want to be inside—even if it's an eclectic art gallery in the "Paris of the South"? Outdoor art is tucked around the sides of buildings and in the alleyways all over downtown. You might miss 'em if you don't know know where to look and you might wreck if you're rubbernecking and driving your car. So, put on your walking shoes. Go ahead. I can wait.

If you're holed up in a downtown hotel, ask someone at the desk to steer you onto Woodfin St. and toward the Asheville Civic Center. At the corner of Woodfin and Broadway turn away from Interstate 240. (If you are coming from some other part of town, look at the map on page 23.) On your left you'll see a beautiful mural on the side of 66 Broadway. The owners of the now defunct Mud Hunter Pottery commissioned local artist Sally Bryenton to create "Simple Gift" in the summer of 2004. The building now houses **Bruisin' Ales**, recently named the *second best beer retailer in the world* by RateBeer Best 2008. IN THE WORLD!(!)

Continue up Broadway and turn left beside the Mellow Mushroom onto Walnut St. Take the first right onto N. Market St. and you're on the last street in Asheville to be brick-paved (back in 1912.) To your left is **Ristorante Vincenzo** with a comedic pair of companions looking out over the streets of Asheville. Vincenzo's was among a handful of restaurants established downtown circa 1989. Having weathered the fads and quirks of time, it's fine dining for any occasion.

Turn right on College St. In the second block on College, you'll practically run into the **Terra Diva** mural finished in February 2005 and disastrously modified in 2008 (perhaps following a graffiti wreck). Yikes it is awful now (see original on back cover).

Continue up College St. for two more blocks and take a right on Haywood St. You'll pass Woolworth Walk on the right which is Asheville's largest venue for local artists. Turn right onto Walnut St. and cross on over to the **Malaprop's Bookstore/Café** side of Walnut. On your left is a bas relief, functional piece of art on the outside of **Zambra's Wine and Tapas Bar**. This window is an intriguing invitation to the unique and evocative atmosphere you'll find inside Zambra's.

Continue walking down Walnut, cross Rankin St. and turn left on Lexington Ave. This block is a multifarious blend of less expensive but delicious eateries and specialty stores on the right side of the street. Over on the left is **Downtown Books and News** with a painting on the north side of the building. The Asheville Mural Project is responsible for this breath of fresh air painted in 2003 -- which highlights the annual migration of monarch butterflies through these mountains (see back cover and page 98). Follow the parking lot to **Heiwa Shokudo**, where an oriental style mural adorns its Woodfin St. side wall. Erin Hunt from Hendersonville is the artist.

One block further north on Lex is the I-240 overpass. The Asheville Mural Project has created a magnificent Lexington Gateway Mural on the stanchions supporting the highway—part of which is pictured on the front cover of this guide.

Backtrack on Lex to Woodfin to return to the starting point of this stroll.

"Simple Gift" by Sally Bryenton

Lazy morning coffee/boutique stroll

This walk will take you through the heart of downtown. The focus will be places to tank up on coffee or tea or some other refreshment and some cool shops to check out.

We'll start out at **Cafe Ello** located at 64 Haywood St. where a lot of locals start their day with fine coffee and the priciest bagels in WNC. (Map p. 17). Moseying south on Haywood you'll pass **Malaprop's Books and Café** on your left, with pastries, coffee, tea and loads of light and heavy reading matter.

Turn right on Battery Park and continue walking up the Flat Iron side of the street. At 18 Battery Park will be **World Coffee**. If looks matter to you in pastries and cakes, you will find a feast for your eyes here, and outdoor seating is plentiful. Speaking of eye-candy, there's a picture frame on the counter displaying a live feed from a roof-top video camera which endlessly scans the Great Smokies to the west. If you prefer intimacy, continue past the coffee bar into the deep recesses of the building and sit beside a window overlooking Wall Street. The back rooms are often empty.

Exiting World Coffee, turn left. In the same block, you will see a shop on the left called **Street Fair.** If you wear earrings, or know someone who does, this is a must-browse. Interesting clothing, jewelry and unique accessories are packed into this little boutique.

Catty-corner from Street Fair sits the Grove Arcade. But the Arcade has a page of its own (see p. 18) and on this walk, take the steps beside Street Fair down to Wall Street. Turning left will take you by many specialty stores. **Beads and Beyond**, **Celtic Way, Paul Taylor Sandals** and **A Far Away Place** are just a few of the interesting places to visit on Wall Street.

Wall Street will take you right back to Battery Park where you take a right, then right again onto Haywood St. Continue past Pritchard Park on your right and take a left on Patton Ave. and follow it for three blocks. You'll pass **Wonderland**, a smoke shop, and **Kress Emporium** on your left, at the corner of Patton and Lexington. Catty-corner you'll see one of Asheville's finest galleries, **16 Patton** (see gallery gawks, p. 55). One door south on Lex, "behind" 16 Patton, is the **French Broad Chocolate Lounge**, with liquid truffle hot sipping chocolates, local draught beer, small-production wines, locally roasted French press coffee, organic loose-leaf teas, locally made ice cream, a collection of small production artisanal chocolate bars.

Staggering back to 16 Patton in the throes of a chocolate buzz, turn right and find **Studio Five Imports**, featuring an ever-changing panoply of strange, vintage and exotic conversation starters. Headed toward the Vance Monument you'll find **Sisters McMullen** on the corner with pastries and baked goods you won't be able to pass up.

If you head north at this point you'll see **Green Sage Coffeehouse and Café** at the corner of College and Broadway.

But if you cross Broadway/Biltmore you'll find **Pack Place**, which houses the **Asheville Art Museum**, the **Colburn Gem and Mineral Museum**, the **Diana Wortham Theater** and the **Health Adventure.**

Proceeding south on Biltmore Avenue, **Mast General Store** is on the west side, along with **Ariel Gallery, Van Dyke Jewelry and Fine Crafts** and **Karmasonics**. On the east side you'll spot **Bellagio Everyday**, the final boutique on this walk-a-bout. It's on the left side of Biltmore next to **Barley's Taproom**.

A few doors down, at 60 Biltmore, is **City Bakery**, great for coffee, breakfast or lunch. Across the street you'll spy **Laurey's**, with its superb menu for a full meal or a tasty bite, and **Mamacita's** offering Cuban/Mexican food with an emphasis on organic and local.

Asheville's CNG fill-em-up on Southside Ave.

Bistros/Coffee Shops

*Bean Werks Coffee & Tea (828-254-7766)
753 Haywood Road (West Asheville)
Beans & Berries (828-254-6969)
165 Merrimon Ave.
City Bakery (828-252-4850)
60 Biltmore
*The Dripolator (828-252-0021)
190 Broadway (to a normal person, this is N. Lexington past I-240)
*Firestorm Café (828 255-8115)
48 Commerce St.
French Broad Chocolate Lounge (828-252-4181)
10 S. Lexington Avenue
Green Light Cafe (828-450-2265)
18 N. Lexington
Green Sage Coffeehouse & Cafe (828-252-4450)
5 Broadway
Izzy's Coffee Den (828-258-2004)
74 N. Lexington Avenue and 373 Haywood Rd., West Asheville
Kismet Café & Coffee House (828-277-0098)
1 Boston Way (Biltmore)
*Malaprop's Books and Café (828-254-6734)
55 Haywood Street
Old Europe (828-255-5999)
13 Broadway
Paris French Bakery (828-252-2315)
1020 Merrimon Ave
Cafe Ello (828-236-0050)
64 Haywood Street
*Sisters McMullen Bakery (828-252-9380)
15 N. Pack Square and 830 Merrimon Ave.
True Confections (3828-50-9480)
Grove Arcade
*West End Bakery (828-252-9378)
757 Haywood Road (West Asheville)
World Coffee (828-258-1058)
18 Battery Park

* particularly recommended by the author

The Urban Trail

You may notice some bronze sculptures scattered throughout the city; a pair of size 13 shoes on the sidewalk, a couple dancing in front of the Civic Center or some livestock that seemed to have lost their way circa the Vance Monument. The shoes belonged to Thomas Wolfe, the dancing couple is meant to evoke Appalachian folk culture and the pigs were, presumably, making their getaway.

Actually, the pigs fell on some very hard times. A driver lost control of his car, headed east on Patton, jumped the extant concrete wall, and knocked the pigs from their pad. Then, after the pigs were reglued, someone stole the piglet. Finally, the ongoing refurbishment of the entire downtown park area required removal of the sow and her companion turkeys for safekeeping. They're back in place now, still headed the wrong way. (The installation is intended to commemorate the drovers' road, whence livestock raisied in the Tennessee Valley were driven through Asheville en route to slaughter in Charleston. The pigs and turkey are headed back toward Tennessee.)

The Urban Trail will take you through downtown where you'll get a history lesson, a trip back in time and 1.7 miles of walking. The whole walk takes an hour and a half or so, and if you take the self-guided tour, you can jump off the trail at any given point, for a meal or shopping.

Self Guided Tours
Tour information is availabe at Pack Place, just south of the Vance Monument at the intersection of Patton Ave. and Biltmore Ave. A cell-phone/mp3 version will be released early in 2011. For information call the Asheville Art Museum. (828) 253-3227

Downtown architectural walk-a-bout

This walk will take you to some of the outlying fingers of central downtown. We'll start on the east end at City/County Plaza and finish up at the Basilica St. Lawrence in the northwest corner. If you have binoculars, bring 'em.

In the 1920s, architect Douglas Ellington had a design for two Art Deco style buildings to be situated side by side. The City Building, with the wedding cake topper, was built in 1928 and combines Art Deco and Beaux Arts elements. The base of the pink-orange brick building is Georgia pink marble and the roof is an octagonal crown of red and green tile.

Asheville is second only to Miami, Florida, in the number of surviving Art Deco buildings.

The city building was a controversial structure in its time and the County Board of Commissioners raised a ruckus over plans for a Deco courthouse. Commissioners settled on a more staid county courthouse by Washington D.C. architects Milburn and Heister. (However, the ruckus between city and county continues.)

Most recently, a thoroughly ugly jail was appended to the back of the courthouse, which entirely blocks the east view of the city hall, making one assume that the commissioners of the 1990s hated Art Deco as vehemently as those pre-Depression grinches.

As the 2005 edition of this guide went to press a grand makeover of Asheville's central park, formerly known as City/County Plaza, had broken ground and should have been completed long ago. It isn't finished in mid-2009. On it goes.

UGLY JAIL

Much of the land between the government buildings and the Vance Monument was left to the community by George Willis Pack in 1901 (see "Daddy's Money," p. 114) to be used "forever ... for the purpose of a public square or park." In 2003 the City Council unanimously approved a plan to sell a large parcel of the park to the Grove Park Inn for development as a high-rise, high-end retail and residential building, but citizens rose up en masse and demanded that the park remain a park.

Sic semper tyrannis!

Then, in 2006, county commissioners sold *another* piece of the park to a developer for a high-rise mixed-use building, and citizens rose up en masse to demand that the park remain a park. The protest was to no avail, but a judge overturned the sale as being in contradiction of Pack's deed. The developer' backed off, decided not to raze tan existing building and created **Pack's Tavern**, an apparently successful beer and bar food joint.

Assuming the makeover is eventually completed—no small effort of faith at this point—roads and parking will be somewhat rearranged. While the essentials of this walk will still be in place, the central grassy area will be renamed the Roger McGuire Green, though much of the "green" has now been paved. (Asheville-Keeping Itself Weird).

Leaving City/County Plaza— Roger McGuire Green, head left (west) on College Street. At the second block take a left onto South Market Street. At the corner of College and Market is Asheville's first skyscraper, the **Jackson Building**. Built in 1924, the brick and terra cotta building is located on the site of Thomas Wolfe's father's stonecutting shop. Use those binoculars if you brought them for a closer look at the gargoyles and other Gothic influenced ornamentation near the top.

Continue south on Market to Eagle St. On the southeast corner is the **Young Men's Institute**.

The YMI is the cultural center of Asheville's African-American community and hosts numerous historic and artistic displays and events each year. George Vanderbilt's supervising architect, Richard Sharp Smith, designed this 19th Century brick and pebbledash Tudor building as a centerpiece of what was then a thriving African-American town center. Subsequent condemnation and municipal development projects obliterated much of that community, as did development of the medical facilities surrounding Mission Hospital, just south of downtown. (See Asheville's Afro-History, page 140).

Hang a right on Eagle Street and walk one block to Biltmore Avenue. Turn right onto Biltmore and continue north until you reach Pack Square.

Let's pause just a moment at the **Vance Monument**, one of Asheville's most famous/infamous landmarks (see "A monument to tolerance," p. 120). The 1896 granite obelisk honors civil war governor and U.S. senator, Zebulon B. Vance. The Vance Monument is another one of Richard Sharp Smith's designs. (Bad day?)

It's worth noting that this monument, dedicated to a man who was passionate about justice (albeit for whites—he was, after all, a slave owner and a Southerner of his times), remains a focal point for justice-seekers today. Peaceful protests for a variety of causes are oftentimes held here and two groups have been demonstrating there weekly since before the misbegotten invasion of Iraq. Many days you can drive by and get a sort of political pulse of the city.

In the early 1990s, the area around the monument presented a somewhat pastoral scene of young people lounging in the grass, some with drums and others with then-astonishing dreadlocks. A hackie-sack marathon was always going on and, at night, the drummers would gather. There was no iron gate around the monument then and the turkeys and pigs hadn't arrived (or departed) yet.

Some of the downtown businesses didn't care for the festive atmosphere, claiming it was bad for business. So, they gated up the monument and exuberant locals migrated to **Pritchard Park**.

With Pack Square on your right, Patton Avenue will be to your left. Head down Patton. One block west you will pass the ornate **Kress Building**, formerly part of the retail chain, now an arts mall and condos.

Continue west another block and you'll see two buildings side by side on the corner of Church and Patton. The four-story **Drhumor Building** (pronounced "drewmore" but colloquially known as the Dr. Humor) is one of the areas finest examples of Romanesque Revival. The limestone frieze and the supporting paired columns were carved by Fred Miles. You can see more of his work at the Basilica St. Lawrence and Biltmore Estate.

Next door is the **S&W Cafeteria**; another Art Deco masterpiece by Douglas Ellington (Richard Sharp Smith must've been really jealous.) The colorfully glazed terra-cotta in a classic geometrical format makes the S&W a gem worth admiring. Don't forget to look up! Recently the S&W has reopened after a long vacancy with **Steak & Wine**, **Corner House** restaurant and **Satchel's Bar**.

If you continue west you will soon come to the **Public Service Building**, originally built for the gas utility corporation but now owned by Public Interest Projects (see "Daddy's Money," p. 114). The building combines Romanesque and Spanish elements in polychrome terra cotta.

If, instead, you turn north on Haywood Street (which will be behind you if you are facing the S&W), you will pass the **Miles Building** on your left. Built in 1901, it features white glazed terra cotta baroque classical cornices (say that fast, for fun). The current owner has gone to phenomenal expense to install copper awnings all the way around the building. Hmm. Interesting effort.

Just past the Miles Building, take a left onto Battery Park Avenue. At the first intersection (Wall Street) you will see the pointy end of the **Flatiron Building**.

Although the construction of buildings with a vaguely tri-angular footprint was considered radical and adventurous in its day, the resulting structure is pretty mundane. Nonetheless, there is a large, somewhat silly sculpture (part of the Urban Trail) at the intersection of Wall Street and Battery Park. This is probably the most photographed flatiron in the world.

In 2009, a drunk driver hit the iron full-tilt-boogey during a high speed chase and moved it fifteen or twenty feet. It has since been returned to its original spot, repainted and ready for more timeless photos. (For no particularly cogent reason, despite having walked by this sculpture hundreds of times, it always, every time, reminds me of the 1970s feminist manifesto. "Don't iron while the strike is hot." I still wear wrinkled shirts in support of Betty, Bella and Gloria.)

After a block, you'll come to the **Grove Arcade**.

Patent medicine magnate E. W. Grove's original intention was a 20 story building, but he died before it was completed and the project fizzled in the financial darkness of the Great Depression. The city itself went bankrupt, a condition which stalled downtown development and resulted in preservation of the Art Deco treasures we see today—buildings of a sort that were routinely destroyed in more prosperous cities during the post-WWII boom times.

Eighty years later, the burst of a housing bubble and collapse of banks, lenders and Wall Street brokerages may have saved Asheville once again from ill-considered development. Three buildings taller than 20 stories were moving forward (on paper) when the financial house of cards blew down and plans to raze and replace chunks of downtown have been placed on hold or, hopefully, abandoned. Cross your fingers.

Final completion of what is now the Grove Arcade came in 1929, after Grove's death, but it never was the skyscraper he envisioned. Griffins stand at the north entrance of this Tudor style structure. Serpentine staircases are a highlight of the interior which has been meticulously renovated. It's definitely worth a walk-through.

Continuing north on Page Avenue will bring you back onto Haywood Street and the **Basilica St. Lawrence**, which will be to your left. Designed by Rafael Guastavino and Richard Sharp Smith, the Basilica is a stunning example of Spanish Baroque Revival style architecture. The limestone figures on each side of the entrance were carved by Fred Miles. The structure was built entirely of brick, stone, tile, and mortar without any wood or iron.

The tiled dome was constructed without any scaffolding by

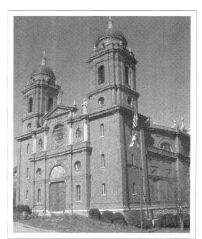

local craftsmen. Instead, the masons would lay about 18 inches of tile per day. The next morning, that section of tile was dry and strong enough to be self-supporting as the workers continued to work on the dome. They would literally stand on their previous day's work until the dome was finished.

Brave Ulysses Books editorial staff
(inserted here at their insistence)

Family Outings

The following are some suggestions for family fun activities in the Asheville area. Many of these recommendations spring from the notion that kids and the out-of-doors just go together naturally; particularly if water is involved.

In town things to do

Climbax Indoor Climbing Center (252-9996)
43 Wall Street
Making its home nestled in the oldest mountain range in the world, Climbax offers **indo**or and outdoor climbing walls suitable for ages 2-82 right downtown! Private guide service is offered whether its a "week-end back-packing trip in virgin forest or Alpine assents of extinct volcanoes."
Tuesday-Thursday 3:30 -10 p.m.
Wednesday-Friday 12 - 10 p.m.
Saturday 10 a.m.- 10 p.m.
Sunday 1 - 6 p.m.

The Health Adventure (254-6373) 1 Pack Square
"A health science museum for children and families dedicated to improving health awareness, promoting wellness lifestyles and increasing science literacy through programs and exhibits." Located in Pack Place on the square in downtown. Let mom take a break with the coffee shop/ boutique walk (see p. 32) while dad takes the kids to the Health Adventure. It's hard to predict who will have the most fun! With a New Adventures Gallery featuring fascinating exhibits from across the country or making a 3-D marshmallow polygon on Annual Pi Day, the museum is open from 10 a.m.- 5 p.m. Tuesday-Saturday.
1 - 5 p.m. on Sundays.
Cost: $5.00 Seniors: $4.00
Children under 2years old: free
www.thehealthadventure.org

• Today the Asheville Art Museum occupies the space originally built to house Pack Memorial Library. This elegant, early 20th century structure is adjacent to Pack Place.

Pack Memorial Library (828-250-4711)

67 Haywood Street

You had planned to go rafting on the Nantahala, but now it's pouring down rain. Although you are apt to get wet anyway in all those rapids, lightning wasn't part of the game plan.

Story-time at Pack Library:

Preschool (ages 3-5) Wednesdays 11 a.m.

Toddlers (ages 18 months-3 years) Thursday 10:30 a.m.

(Other branches of the Asheville-Buncombe Library System have similar programs on different schedules. Give them a buzz.)

Urban Trail (see also page 34)

A great way to tour downtown, this 1.7 mile walking tour visits a series of sculptures commemorating nodal points in the official history of the city. Maps are available as are both guided and self-guided tours (with audio cassettes)/ Call 828-258-0710 or stop by the Asheville Art Museum to learn more.

Not so far from town

Botanical Gardens (828-252-5190)

A 10-acre nature conservatory dedicated to preserving and displaying the native flora of North Carolina. Reed Creek wanders through the park with wonderful bald boulders and smooth bedrock with puddles and tiny waterfalls to play in. A kid's paradise. The Botanical Gardens are located at 151 W.T. Weaver Blvd., next to UNCA.

Saturday morning fun for kids happens once a month at the Botanical Gardens. Usually $1.00/child. Call to register.

Beaver Lake

Go north on Merrimon Avenue approximately three miles past the center of town. A bird sanctuary (did you remember to bring the binoculars?) and a trail that winds around the lake make this a local favorite for dog-walkers, bird-watchers, joggers and walkers. It's beautiful, yet close to town. Unfortunately, swimming is forbidden and boating is limited to dues-paying residents of the surrounding community. But there are lots of places for kids to look for turtles, frogs, salamanders, ducks, mud, wading birds and the rest.

The WNC Nature Center (828-298-5600)

75 Gashes Creek Road

With **indo**or and outdoor exhibits, The Nature Center is a wonderful way to spend the morning or the day—rain or shine. Farm Fun Day,

Hey Day, Reptile Beauty Pageant and Dairy Goat Day are just a few of the special happenings at The Nature Center located at 75 Gashes Creek Road about 15 minutes from downtown. North American River Otters are a favorite attraction as well as the Gray Fox and Red Wolf habitats. Almost all the animals at The Nature Center come there needing medical attention and wouldn't survive in the wild.
Open seven days a week 10 a.m. - 5 p.m.
Seniors- $5.00/Adults- $6.00/Youth (3-15) $4.00/2 and under- free

Lake Julian Park (828-684-0376)
About 20 minutes from Asheville, you can rent paddle-boats and fishing boats for $5.00/hour. Sheltered picnic tables, a play-ground and horse shoes are available. All paddle boats must have one person 16-years old on board.

Adventurous Fast Rivers Rafting (800-438-7238)
Located on the Nantahala River, 1.25 hours from
Asheville. Fun-yaks, "duckies", sit-on-top kayaks and inflatable canoes are available. Call for reservations.

Headwaters Outfitters
(828-877-3106)
Explore the scenic French Broad River just outside of Brevard about one hour southwest of Asheville. Options include three, four, and seven hour self-guided trips. Rates include all equipment and transportation.
Reservations required.

Navitat Canopy Tours (828-626-3700)
Ride a zipline through a forest canopy. Full tilt thrills amidst mountain beauty. Just 20 minutes from downtown.

Southern Waterways (800-849-1970)
Conveniently located in Asheville off the Amboy Rd. exit. Take a guided sunset trip down the French Broad or enjoy a self-guided 7 mile float through the beautiful Biltmore Estate property. Children as young as two years old can participate, providing they weigh at least 35 pounds.

Biking

With Pisgah Forest garnering national recognition for it's trails, there are literally hundreds of miles of single-track trails for biking in the area. All of the places listed below have bike rentals and can point you in the right direction for some fun peddling.

Bio-Wheels (888-881-BIKE)
81 Coxe Ave.
Mountain and leisure bike rentals available. Bio-Wheels offers guided tours as well. Call for reservations.

Hearns Cycling and Fitness (828-253-4800)
28 Asheland Ave.
Established in 1896, offers mountain bike rentals, bike repair, new and used cycles, and lots of gear. Right downtown a block west of Pritchard Park. Very friendly, very helpful staff.

Pro Bikes (828-253-2800) West Asheville
610 Haywood Road
Friendly and helpful, Pro Bikes keeps West Asheville rolling. Guide service available for trail rides, guides trained in emergency medicine, wilderness skills,bike repair and cheerful banter.

Skateboard Park (828-225-7184)
Located at the intersection of Flint Street and Cherry Street about one block north of the Civic Center there is an outdoor skateboard park that consists of a series of interlocking "swimming pools," with curves and ramps and rails.

Restaurants for the family

Here's a list of places offering kid-friendly, relaxed dining where you can all enjoy dinner down-town.

Barley's Taproom (828-255-0504) 42 Biltmore Avenue
While Barley's is a popular local watering hole, I found it to be kid friendly mainly because of the space and the non-smoking area down stairs. It's big enough so that children can walk around a bit and not be in the way of other patrons or the wait staff. It tends to be a bit loud and busy. The pizza is outstanding, the diners and quaffers well behaved, the beer list extensive.

Cats and Dawgs (828-281-8100) 1 Page Ave. (Grove Arcade)
Catfish sandwiches, meat and veggie hot dogs with all the fixin's, varied sides, casual dining indoor or on the sidewalk. Very quick service.

Early Girl Eatery (828-259-9292) 8 Wall Street
Unpretentious atmosphere, really delicious food and very reasonable prices have made this a popular place for dates, business meetings and family meals. Butcher paper on the tables keeps it entertaining for doodlers of all ages and crayons are available upon request.

Heiwa Shokudo (828-254-7761) 87 N. Lexington Avenue
Japanese fare that is very popular with children in my acquaintance. Outdoor seating offers some run-around space in fair weather.

Malaprop's Bookstore and Café (828-254-6734) 55 Haywood Street
With an inviting book nook with pint sized chairs, floor puzzles and stuffed animals, Malaprop's is a kid-friendly space. Although the coffee might not be the thing for the youngsters, smoothies, muffins and other treats are sure to please.

Mamacita's (828-255-8080) 77 Biltmore Ave.
Low key, organic, delicious Mexican food with kid-proof seating and quick service.

Mela (828-225-8880) 70 N. Lexington Ave.
Superb Indian food, excellent and affordable lunch buffet, kids eat free some days.

Laughing Seed Café (828-252-3445) 40 Wall St.
Kid-friendly staff, vegetarian only and very popular. Remodeled with the guidance of a Feng Shui expert and consequently has even better vibes. Or something.

Bus and Segway Tours

Not everybody enjoys walking, and even walkers like to ride now and again. Here are a few ways to tour Asheville on powered wheels.

LaZoom Comedy Tours (828-225-6932)
A slapstick tour of Asheville with a comedy troupe on board. Fun for the whole family. Leaves from the French Broad Food Co-op on Biltmore Ave.
www.lazoomtours.com

Trolley Tours (866-592-8687)
36 Montford Avenue
Buses done up to resemble our fair city's historic trolley cars leave from the Asheville Chamber of Commerce on Montford Avenue just north of Haywood Street (just north of I-240). Drivers offer a steady monologue about the city's history and high points.

Moving Sidewalk Tours (Segway) (828-776-8687)
36 Montford Avenue
Ride a two wheeled stand-up vehicle on a two to three hour narrated tour (led by a wheeled guide). $55

• *Our intrepid police chief, Bill Hogan, astride his trusty Segway during the annual Christmas parade.*

Learn more at: www.movingsidewalktours.com

Let us entertain you— for free!
(a month-by-month guide, repeating events described in first month in which they erupt)

Drum circles – year-round in clement weather

Local drummers gather most Friday evenings in Pritchard Park, in numbers ranging from a handful to several dozen. To many of us, the rhythms and vibrations sent up from the assembly are the very heartbeat of the city. Dancers shimmy and gyrate, passersby stop for a spell and wander on, there is a palpable sense of life that is often absent between the concrete walls and traffic.

A couple of years ago, Blue Meanies with no sense of wonder intervened and demanded that the drummers pay for permits (which they did) and then limited their access to permits. Now it is hit or miss (does that make it syncopated?) and you will find drummers there on some Fridays. When it is happening at full voice it is as marvelous as katydids on an August night or the cacophony of a seabird rookery on a wilderness island. Don't miss it.

Bring oomething to bang on!

APRIL

Westfest

West Asheville's street festival pops up on the fourth Saturday in April. It is a genuinely local event for local folks, and embodies the sense of community that has made West'ville the neighborhood of choice for many young families and small businesses. Music, food, art, fun. See West Asheville info on page 25. www.ashevillewestfest.org

MAY

Mountain Renaissance Adventure Faire

Renaissance faires are set within the period of the Renaissance (about 1454-1610) or the Middle Ages (about 476-1453) and often include elements of fantasy. The Mountain version is the same only in more beautiful surroundings. You'll meet costumed characters who interact with each other and with you. Held the first full weekend in May at Asheville-Buncombe Technical College. www.rennfaire.org

Downtown After Five (828-251-9973)

Once a month, outdoor blues/rock/jam concerts with various pretty-big-name bands. Location varies between Battery Park and North Lexington Ave. Follow your ears. May through September on third Fridays from 5:30-9:00 p.m. Food, libations and port-a-potties available. High spirits kick off the week-end with lively music and a fun time!

Mountain Sports Festival

The Mountain Sports Festival, recently moved to the last weekend in May, features pro and amateur level competitions in paddling, adventure racing, cycling, running, disc golf, climbing, and many other events. Demonstrations and beginner level events in various sports

educate and entertain anyone in attendance. Entry fees for some events, but attendance is free. Center of the action is Carrier Park, on Amboy Road, but events take place throughout the region.
www.mountainsportsfestival.com

JUNE

Concerts on the Quad (828-232-5000)

Family-friendly entertainment on UNCA's campus lawn. Entertainers range from swing bands to story-tellers with puppets to steel drum bands. Bring your lawn chairs, blankets and picnic baskets for an enchanting summer evening.

Monday evenings for the month of June and two weeks in July, 7-8:30 p.m. In case of rain, everybody moves into Lipinsky Auditorium which is adjacent to the quad. A great way to start the work week.

River District Studio Strolls

The warehouses along the French Broad River are home to dozens of artist's studios. (Rent is low, as is the landscape, and some were badly hit by hurricane floods in fall of 2004.) But art, like hope, seems to spring eternal, and creativity continues to flow uphill from the river. Strolls are scheduled in the second week of June and second week of November. (See River District info, page 54)
www.riverdistrictartists.com

Shindig on the Green (828-258-6101)

A well-loved weekly institution for over 35 years, Shindig starts "along about sundown" every Saturday night during July, August and the first weekend in September. Bring a chair or your dancing shoes to Martin Luther King, Jr. Park for some of the areas finest bluegrass and old-time music and clogging.
www.folkheritage.org

Shakespeare in the Park/The Montford Park Players

Since 1973, the Montford Park Players have been presenting free productions of Shakespeare in Asheville, making it the oldest Shakespeare company in North Carolina. If you love Willie's works head for the park on summer weekend nights

To find it from downtown, take Haywood Street away from the shopping district, past the Civic Center, turn north on Montford Avenue, cross the I- 240 bridge, go past the Chamber of Commerce a few blocks and look for an overhead banner. You'll be turning left.
Friday, Saturday, Sunday, 7:30 p.m. June and July.
www.montfordparkplayers.org

Downtown After Five (see May)

JULY

Shakespeare in the Park (see June)

Shindig on the Green (see June)

Downtown After Five (see May)

Bele Chere

A shopping-center-parking-lot-fair on steroids, BC was invented to draw people to Asheville's downtown when it was a moribund ghost town in the late 1970s. Originally featuring local entertainers and local artisans, today it is a parody of itself, heavily advertised outside the region and drawing vast crowds to eat fatty foods, purchase plastic trinkets, get sloshed in public and listen to music. The music is sometimes sublime. The sound is often terrible. There is some good, local art, but it is pretty much lost in the madness. The event is increasingly dominated by mega-corporate sponsors, making it more and more the kind of affair most people come here to *escape*. At this writing the 2009 version is being touted as "downsized." Hmm.

The last weekend in July is a good time NOT to come to Asheville. Bele Chere, by the way, is a meaningless phrase from no known language. If it were French it would mean "moan food," and, may be applicable to those who overindulge in funnel cake.

Chere, Bele?

AUGUST

Downtown After Five (see May)

Shindig on the Green (see June)

Mid-Day Musicals

Popular tunes from Broadway shows, musicals or a particular era in time are performed on a weekly basis by local singers. The season starts the last Thursday in August and runs for six weeks outside Pack Place at 12:30 p.m. It's a 30 minute show well worth your time. A repeat performance of the same repertoire starts the first Saturday of February in Lord auditorium (Pack Library) at 12:30 p.m.

Goombay (828-252-4614)

Goombay is a street celebration of African-American and African-Caribbean cultures held annually since 1982. South Market and Eagle Street are closed off to cars and booths featuring arts and crafts, jewelry and ethnic food appear. Music, dancing, drumming and children's activities too. This festival happens the last weekend in August.

www.ymicc.org/goombay.html

SEPTEMBER

Mid-Day Musicals (see August)

Shindig on the Green (see June)

Lexington Avenue Arts & Fun Festival

A truly local celebration of the arts, LAAFF is, in many ways, what Bele Chere started out to be. Poor Bele Chere ate too many funnel cakes, drank too many beers and lost her youthful figure. LAAFF helps locals remember why they used to love Bele Chere. Held the first weekend in September.

www.laaff.org

OrganicFest

An annual celebration of organic, local food and healthy lifestyles, OrganicFest happens about the second weekend in September. Staged by Pure Food Partners, the event features music, politics, natural/organic vendors and a Pollinator Parade—children dressed up as butterflies and other insects.

www.organicfest.org

Downtown After Five (see May)

Fiesta Latina (828-252-4614)

As the name suggests, Fiesta Latina is a celebration of the Hispanic/Latino community in WNC. Held in mid-September, this street fiesta features ethnic food, traditional and current music, and bilingual exuberance.

www.ymicc.org/fiesta_latina.html

Greek Festival (828-253-3754)

Sponsored by the Holy Trinity Greek Orthodox Church since 1986, the event is a Greek food lover's holiday. Traditional music and dance combine with children's events and family fun in City/County plaza. Last weekend in September.

Gallery Crawls: Center City Art Walks (828-258-0710)

Watching Asheville unfurl on a week-end evening is delightful—there's a certain buzz in the air. An intimate downtown event, the gallery crawls happen every other month from Spring to Fall starting at 5 p.m. of a Friday and winding down at 8 p.m. Get a brochure from any participating gallery or the Chamber of Commerce and walk around. Many places have wine or light refreshments on hand.

NOVEMBER

River District Studio Strolls (see June)

Photo of Cold Mountain compared to painting provides explanation of why the author is taking painting lessons in the River District.

The Paris
of the
South?

Art
Food
Music

Now we're talking Art

Since the end of the 19th century, when George Vanderbilt brought in artisans and artists from various centers of civilization to build his vast mansion just south of Asheville, this area has been chock full of art. Further back, of course, there was the craft and decorative work of the indigenous people and European settlers. Along the way, geologists discovered that the soil and rock hereabouts is laden with pottery precursors including various clays and feldspar. Potters being easier to transport than clay, artisans flocked to these WNC mountains. Biltmore Industries, the John C. Campbell Folk School (in Brasstown) and Penland School heightened awareness of this region's crafts and turned out well-trained artists.

Then, in the 1980s, Buncombe County and Asheville City governments made a conscious decision to advance arts for the benefit of local citizens, both for education and economic development. Today, the arts are a major factor in the local economy. And lots of people come to gawk.

The post-recession economy has been tough for galleries and a handful mentioned in earlier editions of this book have gone under. Others are reliably rumored to be skating on thin financial ice. So gawk all you like, but, for the artists, please buy something!

Smack in the middle of town is the superb **16 Patton Avenue** at the corner of South Lexington and Patton. The name of the gallery and the address are one and the same. This gallery carries classic and contemporary fine art including figurative and abstract works, often presenting thematic shows featuring numerous local artists. Exiting the gallery, turn right until you get to Biltmore Avenue where you take another right turn.

Across Biltmore you'll see Pack Place, home to both the **Asheville Art Museum** and the Gallery at Pack Place with continually changing exhibits. Heading south on the west side of Biltmore you'll come to **Ariel Gallery**. Ariel includes weavers, bookmakers, marblers, sculptors and glassblowers, primarily from the Toe River area, surrounding the **Penland School**. This is high-end craft work of the first caliber. A half block along you'll find a newcomer, **2**.

Next, cross the street. Abutting the south side of the **Fine Arts Theater** you'll find **Blue Spiral 1 Gallery** at 38 Biltmore Avenue. In this 14,000 square feet of space, 75 permanent artists and over 28 annual exhibitions by southeastern artists are displayed. You may well get lost in this stunning three-level gallery so think about feeding that meter again. Next door, and under the same ownership is **Bellagio Everyday** (art to wear). Continue south on Biltmore another block to the stunning **Haen Gallery** with its ever-changing displays of contemporary painting and sculpture. Another half-block, just past City Bakery, find **American Folk Art & Framing** at 64 Biltmore Avenue with a bubble machine spewing forth to lure bubble-lovers. Americans love a bubble be it housing, internet or oil.

On the north side of downtown (see map p. 23), we'll start at 106 North Lexington Avenue (near the I-240 mural pictured on the cover of this book) at **Crucible Glassworks**: "where the art of glass meets the art of shopping." Learn about this ancient art while you watch hot glass demonstrations. From the fiery furnace, to the glory hole, to the annealing oven, see a vast array of colors come alive in functional and aesthetic pieces. Exiting Crucible Glassworks, go south on Lexington until you reach Woodfin Street. Turn east on Woodfin and walk uphill past two alleys until you hit Broadway (the second "alley" is **Carolina Lane**, see page 59).

Heading north on Broadway, on the left, around the middle of the block will be the **Black Mountain College Museum & Art Center**. Steeped in history, this museum is dedicated to exploring the legacy of Black Mountain College, the world's most acclaimed experimental educational community. A partial list of teachers and alumni includes people such as **Willem** and **Elaine de Kooning**, **Robert Rauschenberg**, **Josef** and **Anni Albers**, **Jacob Lawrence**, **Merce Cunningham**, **John Cage**, **Cy Twombly**, **Kenneth Noland**, **Ben Shahn**, **Franz Kline**, **Arthur Penn**, **Buckminster Fuller**, **M.C. Richards**, **Francine du Plessix Gray**, **Charles Olson**, **Robert Creeley** and **Dorothea Rockburne.** Just a bit further and you'll spy the **L.O.F.T.** (lost objects, found treasures), one of those hard to define shops that is partly art, partly craft, partly gift, partly Asheville.

At the corner of Broadway and Walnut Street, the bowling-ball-and-stone wall encircling the patio at a chain pizza restaurant is worth a look. Hook left past the bowling ball wall on Walnut, then walk two short blocks and turn right onto North Spruce Street, you will find the **Appalachian Craft Center**. The craft center is a treasure trove of traditional mountain crafts and hand made items. Pottery, quilts, and handmade rugs are just a few of the handiworks you'll find here.

Continue south on N. Spruce to College Street and hang a right. Walk two blocks to cross Broadway and continue downhill to North Lexington. Hang another right.

BoBo Gallery at 22 N. Lex is more a bar than an art destination, but they feature current local art on the walls.

Continuing north across Walnut, find **Chatsworth Art & Antiques**, with an emphasis on the latter. You can continue north on Lex to your starting place (in which case, cross the street to **Downtown Books and News** and check out the mural on the north wall) or back track a few steps to Walnut and go uphill to Carolina Lane. Turn left into what looks like an alley and find **Fresh**, which features up and coming ceramic artists. Along the way, check out the murals and graffiti. Continuing on Carolina Lane takes you back to Woodfin where a left turn will return you to the start of the walk.

On the west side of downtown, a short stroll down College and Haywood Streets includes a string of galleries, and you can then loop back through the Grove Arcade, so plan on parking in the vicinity (see parking p. 13). Our first stop will be where College Street and Patton Avenue converge, on the west end of Pritchard Park (see map, p. 22). Start with **A Boy and his Dog, Fine Art**, at 89 Patton. Owned by David Todd, the gallery was previously located in Key West, and moved here in 2008. Todd has owned the gallery for over twelve years and opened multiple galleries in Florida. His Dalmatian, Simon, spends many days in the gallery greeting art lovers. Going east find another relative newcomer, **Aesthetic Gallery,** at 6 College Street, with a mix of international arts and crafts. Exiting Aesthetic, go left just a few doors east, down to 16 College Street to the **Asheville Gallery of Art**. An intimate, cooperative gallery since 1988, it was one of the first galleries in Asheville and has remained in its original location. The 29 member co-op features regional painters in genres from representational to abstract.

Continue east as you leave the Asheville Gallery of Art and walk on to Haywood Street and hang a left. On the right side of Haywood is the **Woolworth Walk**, a renovated old Woolworth's store. The retro diner inside is original, complete with red trim and stools at the counter. This is Asheville's largest venue for local artists and has a bit of everything from jewelry to hand-made journals, scarves, purses and even neon.

Headed north on Haywood you'll pass two prime sources for artistic material. On your right, **EarthGuild** offers a wide selection of craft materials and on your left, **True Blue Art** provides top-notch supplies for two dimensional fine art.

Further along you'll find **Mobilia** (arty housewares, recently moved a half block east on Walnut) and **Origami Ink** and **Bender Glass** just past Malaprop's Books and Café.

Stepping out of Bender, you will see **Jewels That Dance** just up the way. As much a gallery as a jewelry store, those fascinated by artwork in metal and precious stones will be spellbound by the work displayed there. Continuing north on Haywood, past the Asheville Civic Center and in front of the Basilica St. Lawrence, hang a left on Page Avenue. (As we go to press, the streets at this intersection are slated for major reconfiguration, so your left turn may be renamed, but any left at this point will get you where you want to go.) Ahead you will spy the Grove Arcade, but before you cross Page, walk one door past Captain's Bookshelf to a new gallery which featured a glass show and no visible name as this book went to press.

The Arcade boasts a wealth of galleries, some in that grey area between gallery and gift shop. You decide. Current "arty" shops there include Asheville NC Home Crafts (all local artisans), The Blue Ridge Textillery (regional crafts and textiles), Mission At the Grove (Arts & Crafts replicas, some antiques) and Mountain Made (an all regional offering from the non-profit Mountain Bizworks).

A short drive north from downtown at 365 Merrimon Ave. you'll find **Blackbird Frame & Art**. Don't be fooled by the name— yes they are a frame shop (with a frame manufacturing shop at another location), but they hand an extensive art collection, representing more than 20 regional artists.

Vincent van Gogh's ear, for you ear fanciers.

Carolina Lane

Asheville's inner fringe

Between Lexington Avenue and Broadway, between Walnut and Woodfin Streets, runs Carolina Lane. (see map p. 23) This short and relatively nondescript street has had a disproportional effect on turn-of-the-twenty-first century life in this city. The French Broad Food Co-op found its first home on this alley, back in the 1970s. In those days, Stone Soup, a collective restaurant, held forth just around the corner in the old Pure gas station where a chain pizza restaurant is presently located. (Stone Soup's legacy continues at uncounted other local businesses today.) The co-op not only continues as a local community institution, but helped spawn Carolina Organic Growers which makes North Carolina organic food available statewide.

In the 1990s the legendary Green Door performance space, at 14 Carolina Lane, hosted an explosion of creative effort. Poetry slams, songwriters' circles, plays (both legit and experimental), dances and exhibits stretched the boundaries of art and entertainment in Asheville. A few alumni of that nexus include: Betsy Ball (The Sequins), Cecil Bothwell (*My Brother's Koin*; *The Icarus Glitch*; *The Prince of War: Billy Graham's Crusade for a Wholly Christian Empire*; *Pure Bunkum: Reporting on the life and crimes of Buncombe County Sheriff Bobby Lee* Medford; et. al.); Silent Partners— Hillarie Burke (*Girls Wear Shirts*) and Connie Schrader (*A Sense of Dance*); Laura Hope-Gill (*Nothing Personal*); David Hopes (*Bird Songs of the Mesozoic*; *A Dream of Adonis*; et. al.); David LaMotte (*Spin; Change*; et. al.); Laura Moran (*Live Bait*, et. al.); Jim Navé (The Artist's Way; The Writer's Workshop); Glenis Redmon (*Backbone*, et. al.); Allan Wolf (slam-master, *The Blood Hungry Spleen, New Found Land*; *Zane's Trace*; *More Than Friends*; et. al.). Nationally known performers included Ray McNeice, Patricia Smith, Michael Brown, Marc Smith, Gary Glazner, David Wilcox, the London Poetry Slam Team, Juanita Tobin and Maggie Estep, to name a few.

Non-performers who made the Green Door stuff happen and continue to contribute to the local arts scene include Lee Lancaster and Ginger West. Three Green Door performers who have passed on, in relative youth, deserve mention: Grant Hasty, Christine Lassiter and Pat Storm all died much too early. Much, much too early.

Carolina Lane is the canvas for many local mural and graffiti artists and offers a constantly changing scriptorum for local activism. Check it out! WAS: Like the graffiti says, the Green Door "was ..."

The River Arts District

Like many river fronts, Asheville's was once home to major industries that needed water, power and transportation. (While the French Broad River falls too fast to be commercially navigable, the railroad here, as everywhere, followed the river valley as the path of least resistance.) Once a bustling commercial district, the area now called the River Arts District has seen more than its share of hard times. In 1916 and 2004 it was drowned by flood waters, in 1986 a fire completely destroyed a significant section (much of the former Asheville Cotton Mill) and in 1929 it collapsed, along with the rest of the economy, into the Great Depression. Asheville didn't recover financially from the Depression until the 1970s, when it finally paid off debts incurred in the throes of that miasma.

Many of the buildings in the River Arts District sat empty for periods of years, or were used as inexpensive storage space for businesses whose offices were elsewhere. Cheap space, of course, is an artist's dream, and beginning in the 1980s, artists began to collocate in a roughly triangular area circumscribed by Clingman Avenue, Riverside Drive and Haywood Road.

The easiest way for a newcomer to get to the River Arts District from downtown Asheville is to start at Pritchard Park and drive north on Haywood Street past the Civic Center and Basilica St. Lawrence, on past the Three Brothers Restaurant and the Buncombe County Sheriff's Department, on and on to the traffic light at Patton Avenue. Cross Patton and Haywood Street magically becomes Clingman Avenue. Follow Clingman to the **Silver Dollar Diner** and turn **left** just before the **Grey Eagle Music Hall** (Asheville's best listening room). Confusingly, this left turn puts you on Clingman again—at this intersection the main road you just left reverts to Haywood, only now it is Haywood Road, which continues into West Asheville.

Proceed past the Grey Eagle (on your right) to a five way intersection, which is where this tour begins. Just before the intersection, grab breakfast or lunch at the **Clingman Cafe** which, together with the **Odyssey Center for the Ceramic Arts,** is to your left, facing Clingman. **Highwater Clays**, a major ceramic supplier that started right here in Asheville, recently moved its clay warehouse and retail store a bit further up Riverside Drive. **Judson Gerard Studios** is adjacent to the Cafe The former warehouse has been converted into additional clay studios on Clingman Avenue. Straight ahead through the intersection, find the Fine Arts League, a classical art school, and a new suite of bright pastel studios just being completed as this goes to press. A hard right at the 5-way puts you on Roberts Street (more studios, including several in The Wedge. The next spoke of the wheel is Lyman Street, which crosses the railroad tracks. There is free parking on the right, just before the tracks, and all of the River District studios are within a reasonable walking distance from this point. (The following directions will take you on a loop back to this point.)

Across the tracks and fronting on Riverside Drive, you'll find the **Warehouse Studios**, currently home to six painters and one quilter. Note the small white line to the left of the door for **Riverlink** (our local waterway preservation non-profit). It denotes the high water mark of the 1916 flood. The 2004 high water mark was six to 10 feet below that of the Great Flood. Next to the Warehouse you'll find **Curve Studio**, home to a glass blower, wood worker, photographer and quilter. These buildings have housed a paint and body shop, a rock club, the M.T. Mitchell Distillery (1907) and an oil company over the past century. Proceeding northwest on Riverside and ducking under the Riverlink Bridge (Haywood Road) you next find **The Cotton Mill**, a remnant of the large manufacturing complex which housed The Asheville Cotton Mill, starting in 1896. The Mill now houses a clay studio as well as a variety of other art forms including dancers, flute makers and painters. Internationally recognized landscape artist John Mac Kah is among the artists who work in the Cotton Mill.

Continuing on Riverside and hanging a right on Roberts Street, you'll find the tiny **Railside Studios**, offering mixed media. You'll discover that Roberts Street curves to the right and then parallels Riverside Drive as you head southeast to the intersection with Haywood Road, where you'll find the **Phil Mechanic Studios**. A former warehouse, built circa 1925, it is now populated by artists working in multiple media.

Across Haywood Road from the Mechanic studios, a group of buildings on Roberts Street once served as a commercial produce market. Renamed **The Wedge** by it's former owner, steel sculptor John Payne (who died in 2008), it now houses studios dedicated to a wide variety of art forms as well as the **Wedge Brewery**, Asheville finest local beer crafter with pub and pub grub.

Across the street from the Wedge are the Roberts Street Studios (metal, mixed media, glass, painting), built in the mid-20th century. Continuing on Roberts Street, you will come back to your car if you parked across the tracks from **Warehouse Studios**. Just a mile down Lyman (after crossing the tracks, it hooks left), you'll find the **Candlestation**. In the late 19th century, the building now known as the Candlestation was built to house the Asheville Tannery. Today's tenants work in pottery, wood, mixed media and fiber.

Restaurants

Asheville has more restaurants per capita than ... hmmm. You hear that a lot. Depending on your source— you might be told, more than any U.S. city other than San Francisco, or possibly Portland, or maybe it's Lexington (a whole slew of cities claim to have the most, attempting to win tourists' hearts via their stomachs).

At last count there were more than 600 restaurants in Buncombe County. We do have the highest number of vegetarian restaurants per capita of any city in the U.S. according to PeTA.

With all that competition, it's tough for a restaurant to "make it" here. We've seen a lot of eating establishments come and go over the years (sometimes less than a year) and it's hard to predict which ones will float and which ones won't. Here is a list of restaurants that have been here a while which I regard as a cut above the rest.

Hey, it's just my opinion, but when you write a book you can be selective too. The restaurants are listed in alphabetical order with some information that I hope will help you decide exactly what strikes your culinary fancy If you have children with you and this list leaves you clueless, please see p. 45 for my list of kid friendly restaurants.

Location descriptions of north, east or central are relative to downtown, all of these places, unless otherwise noted, are within walking distance from any downtown parking area. I like all of these places or I wouldn't mention them here, but asterisks * indicate author faves among the faves.

*Asheville Pizza and Brewing Co. (828-254-1281)   north
675 Merrimon Ave.

Known locally as the "Brew'n'View," what's not to like?— pizza joint, brewpub and movie theater. Although the pizza has walked off with the numero uno spot for many years in a row in local "best-of" publications, Jasmine's Artsy Spin Dip, the chicken fingers and the spinach burger are just as wonderful. The menu is loaded with a variety of sandwiches, salads, pasta and munchies. There's a moderately priced lunch buffet offered daily from 11 a.m. to 3 p.m. Pizzas may be customized with a peppercorn or toasted sesame crust, soy cheese or fat free cheese.

Movies are second-run with couches, comfy seats and tables for your food and beverages. At two bucks for a flick, delicious food very moderately priced and a variety of brews on tap, this place rocks for bargain date night, family entertainment or the "gotta-have-pizza-and-a-movie" bug. In-house beers include a dark Rook Porter, the crisp, hoppy Shiva I.P.A. (India Pale Ale) and Houdini ESP (Extra

Special Pale ale). (See Pub Prowl, p. 74)

To top it all off, the Brew and View is a huge supporter of local charitable efforts. This business typifies the consciousness that makes so many people eager to make Asheville home.

*Asheville Brewing Company (828- 255-4077)   central
Coxe Avenue

The Brew & View's brewing operation has blossomed into a brew pub and restaurant in its own right. The menu runs to pub grub and, of course, great pizza. ABC has become the venue-of-choice for a raft of progressive political groups including Obama campaign meetings during 2008 and ongoing Drinking Liberally gatherings on Thursday nights.

Barley's Taproom (828-255-0504)   central
42 Biltmore Avenue

A lively, local favorite for all ages, Barley's serves up some of the best pizza in town—by the slice or by the pie. The spinach salad, garlic knots and a pint of cool brew is a perennial favorite for a light supper.

Barley's offers more than 90 kinds of beer with 46 being on tap and several varieties by local micro-breweries as well. Decisions can be tough, but the friendly waitstaff will be glad to assist or let you taste. The downstairs is smoke free until 10:00 p.m. and the upstairs has darts, pool and ashtrays all hours. Live music frequently. (See Pub Prowl, p. 74)

*Bouchon (828-350-1140)   central
62 North Lexington Avenue

Want a dark, romantic creperie to feast with your sweetheart? How about some good French wine and some mojo rousin' gypsy music after dinner? Bouchon is the perfect place to court your honey or have a celebratory night out on the town with friends. Courtyard dining is available March through October, weather permitting. Bon appetit!

City Bakery (828-254-4289)   central
88 Charlotte St. and 60 Biltmore Ave.

Scones, vegan pastries, decadent danishes and the organic coffee's pretty good too. Brought to you by the same folks that whipped up The Laughing Seed Cafe and Jack of the Wood, the City Bakery provides bread to many of the local health food stores. Deli style sandwiches, pizza, quiche, rustic foccocia and homemade soups round out the lunch/dinner offerings. Street-side picture windows make a warm reading nook with the morning sun streaming through. Warning:the scones are addictive.

**Early Girl Eatery (828-259-9292)   central
8 Wall Street

Home-style comfort food served alongside newfangled cuisine like vegan sausage, scrambled tofu and multi-grain pancakes. The Southern Breakfast with country ham or bacon is a real bargain and everything from the granola to the sausage is made from scratch. You can get breakfast all day, too. Most food is organic with an emphasis on local. Beef is grass-fed and includes Asheville's best cheeseburger. Poultry and pork is pastured. Lunch items such as black-eyed pea cakes fill out the lunch/dinner menu along with sandwiches, salads and soups. Early Girl Eatery is an exceptional value with amazing food and reasonable prices. Whether your culinary bent leans toward carnivorous or vegan, the Early Girl has something for everyone on their menu.

The Flying Frog (828-254-9411)   central
1 Battery Park Avenue

Put on that red dress and make a reservation for an exceptional dinner downtown underneath the The Frog Bar and Deli at 1 Battery Park. The Flying Frog is perhaps the most elegant restaurant in Asheville. Menu selections vary from traditional to innovative with offerings from Indian, German and Japanese cuisines. Where else, in this little town, will you find a wine list that runs up to $2,000 per bottle? The bar/deli features sidewalk seating and is open for lunch.

*Heiwa Shokudo (828-254-7761)   central
87 North Lexington Avenue

Excellent and varied Japanese menu which leans heavily toward seafood. Dine inside or out (weather permitting). Tiny and sometimes jammed at regular meal times (particularly when it is rainy or cold) you can order anything as a take-out if the wait seems over long. Don't miss the purple pickles.

Jack of the Wood (828-252-5445)   central
95 Patton Avenue

Jacks has an intimate, neighborhood feel while being right smack dab in the center of town. Large wooden tables and a dim interior give a cozy Celtic flavor to this popular pub. The traditional Irish favorites of Beef Stew, Sheperd's Pie, Fish and Chips and the popular bread, cheese and chutney plate are menu mainstays while soups and salads round out the high quality pub fare.

Celtic, swing and bluegrass bands frequently perform there and it's a smoke-free establishment. Home of organic Green Man Ales, you'll also find a wide selection of imports on tap by the pint.

*Jerusalem Garden Cafe (828-254-0255)   central
78 Patton Avenue.

With a dependable selection of mid-eastern fare and very reasonable prices, Jerusalem Garden does a steady business at both lunch and dinner. The back room features swaying draperies, floor cushions and low tables for those who prefer to eat in a mid-east atmosphere. Belly dancers wiggle through from time to time, and there's live music on weekends. Stop by in the morning for a traditional southern breakfast to get your own belly dancing with delight.

Kanpai Sushi Thai(828-225-8885)   central
3 Biltmore Avenue

Best downtown sushi according to my favorite food reviewer. Best Japanese food in town according to my favorite junior food reviewer. The menu is interesting and prices reasonable.

Laughing Seed Cafe (828-252-3445)   central
40 Wall St.

Asheville's oldest extant veggie foodery. If you've never been to a vegetarian restaurant before and are a bit hesitant, this is the place to go. If you missed out on the Pub Prowl (p. 74) or Jack of the Wood, local organic Green Man ales are available here. Vegetarian only.

**Limones (828) 252-2327   central
13 Eagle Street

Fabulous cocktails (don't miss the Margarita Caliente) and gloriously inventive Mexican cuisine. One of Asheville's finest.

Lobster Trap (828-350-0505)   central
35 Patton Avenue
    Great seafood and steaks and live entertainment. Tasting good! Most amusing wine list in WNC.

Lucky Otter (828-253-9595)   west asheville
630 Haywood Road
    Behemoth burritos, quesadillas, soups, chili,tacos, huevos rancheros—somehow not what you'd expect from a restaurant named after a local mammal. Most unique print ads in town.

*Mamacita's (828-255-8080)   central
77A Biltmore Avenue
    An emphasis on local, organic ingredients means the food is high quality and fresh, and the menu is piled high with tasty Mexican/Latin options. Try the fish tacos! Informal and reasonably priced.

*The Market Place (828-252-4162)   central
20 Wall Street

Established as a world class restaurant and applauded by *The New York Times, Food and Wine, Bon Appetit, Southern Living* and *Wine Spectator,* The Market Place utilizes the best organic and local ingredients for an ever-evolving menu. Entrees at press time included Moroccan Lamb Stew with chick peas and olives and a Carolina Trout stuffed with portobello mushrooms, spinach and onions along with other delicacies. Hot and cold appetizers are available with an innovative twist and wines are carefully selected to be paired with the day's menu.

Mayfel's(828-252-8840   central
22 College St.
    New Orleans style American food served **indo**ors or out, overlooking Pritchard Park. A fine place to eat when the drum circle is in full voice.

Mela (828-225-8880)   **central
70 Lexington
     Superb North and South Indian food with a popular lunch buffet that is scrumptious and very reasonably priced. The food is really, really good. Really good. The only downside is that the acoustics are terrible, so when the place is busy it is also loud. Not for an intimate dinner, but not to be missed. Best mid-priced dinners in town.

New French Bar (828-254-5070)   **central**
12 Biltmore Avenue
     Now serving lunch and dinner and a popular spot for night owls to gather. The courtyard in the back is quiet and well away from the bustle of the sidewalk. The bar room on the street side is excessively smoky most of the time, but the back dining room is well ventilated. Enjoy the sweet potato ravioli, a shrimp quesadilla or the asiago chicken. Sunday brunch features a make-your-own Bloody Mary Bar.

Nine Mile (828-505-3121)   **central
233 Montford Avenue
     Jamaican with flair. Warm atmosphere and easy parking just a few blocks north of downtown in Montford. (If you can find the Visitors' Center, just keep driving north.) Excellent selection of local beer. Friendly staff. Best new restaurant in 2008.

*Over Easy Cafe (828-236-3533)   **central**
32 Broadway
Great place for breakfast with an interesting menu and funky -mod décor. Expect a wait on weekends, this place is tiny and very popular.

Rosetta's Kitchen (828-232-0738)   **central
111 Broadway (or 114 North Lexington Avenue)
     Climb the stairs up to Rosetta's from Lexington and meet Asheville—facial hardware, tattoos, green hair and all. Choose from menu items like smashed potatoes, sweet potato fries and avocado sandwiches. Rosetta always has a pot of greens steaming and this is the place to go for delicious, inexpensive, vegetarian or vegan eats. The patio is charming for dining and you can find a diversity of local art on the inside walls. Serves food VERY late.
Vegetarian only.

*Salsa Mexican-Caribbean (828-252-9805)   central
23 Broadway ave.

If your taste-buds yearn for something as exotic as wild boar or roasted pumpkin with goat cheese, or a shot of Hector's famously fiery salsa, then Salsa's is the place to go. This picture is from the old location (1994-2010), with the move to Broadway just announced as we go to press. Definitely a worth-the-wait place where you will definitely have to wait at peak dining hours, the food presentation is as lovely as the local artwork on the walls. It's a bustling, funky place. Bring your biggest appetite or a doggy bag.

*Sazerac(828-376-0031)   central
20 Broadway
Dim and intimate bar downstairs and cloistered outdoor dining on the roof make this a romantic favorite. The menu offers unlikely and surprisingly tasty cocktails and gourmet food. Really excellent and interesting.

*Sunny Point Cafe & Bakery (828-252-0055)   west asheville
626 Haywood Road
If you're in Westville at breakfast time be sure to stop in at Sunny Point. A diverse menu with lots of options and outdoor seating for clement weather. Like other dining hotspots, expect a wait at

peak times, but hang out and enjoy the garden.

Suwana's Thai Orchid(828-281-8151)   central
11 Broadway

    Asheville's newest Thai. Getting great reviews.

*Table (828-254-8980)   central

    Elegant presentation, a unique wine list and a hip urban décor in an intimate setting make this one of the best options for an "important" dinner. They call themselves a "market driven seasonal New American Restaurant." Whatever, it's good.

*Tingle's Cafe (828-255-4000)   central
27 Broadway

    Tingle's is a resurrection of a cafe first opened in 1918 and which operated for 32 years in the current location. Restoration of the original is gorgeous, and the restaurant offers reasonably priced traditional fare. The ginger ale, for example, is stirred up fresh from ginger simple syrup, bitters, soda, shaken in a cocktain shaker, with fresh ginger grated over the top, and garnished with a mint leaf.

Tupelo Honey Cafe (828-255-4863)   central
12 College Street

    Traditional southern fare with a Big Easy twist, Tupelo serves up lunch and dinner with breakfast around the clock. Hours vary so call ahead, but Tupelo is reliably open on Fridays and Saturdays 'till mid-night for the night-owl munchies. The fluffy biscuits are pitch-perfect with a dollop of honey or underneath Eggs Betty, a brunch favorite. Sidewalk dining makes for great people watching near Pritchard Park. Very popular, you can expect a wait at regular meal times.

Vincenzo's Bistro and Ristorante (828-254-4698) central
Market Street

    Vincenzo's is located on historic Market Street and is Asheville's premiere Northern Italian, Continental restaurant. Since 1990, it's been a favorite place to take that special someone for an exceptional night out. Upstairs is the "ristorante" with a comfortable, yet elegant, white tablecloth dining room. The Bistro features live music every night.

Vincenzo's building served as a City morgue during the 1918 influenza epidemic, was home to Asheville's first vegetarian eatery in the 1970s, and was the first location for Mark Rosenstein's Marketplace Restaurant (see above).

*West End Bakery (828-252-9378)   west asheville
757 Haywood Road

West End offers organic and natural baked treats from bread to scones to the city's best sticky buns, as well as soup and sandwiches at lunch time. With a magazine rack full of intellectual and progressive titles, the latest local free publications and a meeting room free to community groups, this bakery aims for the head as well as the tummy, and scores.

*Westville Pub (828-225-9782)   west asheville
777 Haywood Road

Westville Pub has great pub grub and some surprises too, in vegetarian and seafood offerings. With a dozen micro and import brews on tap, plus dozens of bottled beers, beer is not a problem. Wednesdays are all-you- can-eat lasagna affairs and Friday always features a seafood special. Check out the listing under music (p. 77) for more about this West Asheville fave.

*Zambra Wine & Tapas (828-232-1060)   **central**
85 Walnut St.

Stepping down into Zambra's tapas restaurant you'll be transported to a romantic taste of Portugal with Moroccan influences and fine Spanish wines. Allow plenty of time to enjoy a leisurely meal. This place is an evening unto itself. In the southern region of

Spain, where tapas originated, the walk from tapas bar to tapas bar with friends (which is still popular on the weekends) is as much about socializing as the food and drink. Two to three plates should be sufficient for one person, but the whole idea is to share plates, sampling a bit of this and that. The waitress will be glad to leave the menu with you so you can order more. The tapas are imaginative and delicious with fresh combinations and the interior is one of the most creative and beautiful dining rooms in Asheville. Designed with moorish influences, the interior is accented with plush pillows and comfortable settings with a few semi-private rooms toward the back of the restaurant. Entertainment ranges from jazz to flamenco on varying nights. If you don't eat dinner here, at least stop in a for a glass of port or dessert—you'll be glad you did.

Shadows inside the historic Grove Arcade and a street figure at the corner of Broadway and Walnut.

Sunday Brunch

Bier Garden (285-0002)
46 Haywood St.
Noon - 3 p.m.
***Early Girl Eatery** (259-9292)
8 Wall St.
9:00 a.m. - 3 p.m. Saturdays too.
Frog Bar and Deli (254-9411)
1 Battery Park
11:30 a.m. - 3 p.m.
Jerusalem Garden Cafe (254-0255)
78 Patton Ave. 1
0:30 a.m. - 3 p.m.
Laughing Seed Cafe (252-3445)
40 Wall St.
10:00 a.m. - 2 p.m.
The Lobster Trap (350-0505)
35 Patton Ave.
11 a.m. - 3 p.m.
Mayfel's (252-8840)
22 College Street
9 a.m - 3 p.m.
New French Bar (254-5070)
12 Biltmore Avenue
10:30 a.m. - 4 p.m.
***Rosetta's Kitchen** (232-0738)
111 Broadway
11:30 a.m. - 3 p.m.
***Westville Pub** (225-9782)
777 Haywood Road
11 a.m. - 3 p.m.

Breakfast all day

***Early Girl Eatery** (259-9292)   8 Wall St.
The Over Easy Breakfast Cafe (236-3533)
32 Broadway (until 2 p.m.)
***Sunnypoint Café and Bakery** (252-0055) 626 Haywood Road
Tupelo Honey Cafe (255-4863)   12 College St.
Beans & Berries (828) 254-6969   165 Merrimon Ave.

* author faves

Ice Cream
The Hop (828-252-8362)
507 Merrimon Avenue & 721 Haywood Rd. (West Asheville)
Kamm's Kustard (828-225-7200)
1 Page Avenue (Grove Arcade)
*Ultimate Ice Cream (828-296-1234)
1070 Tunnel Road (a little way east, but worth the drive)

Dessert
Chocolate Fetish (828-258-2353)
36 Haywood Street
Cookies by Design (828-253-9455)
23 Haywood Street
*French Broad Chocolate Lounge
2 South Lexington Ave.
***Short Street Cakes (828-505-4822)
225 Haywood Rd. Best cakes in WNC!
***Sugar Momma's Cookies (828-251-7277) BEST COOKIES IN
ASHEVILLE, NO QUESTION WHATSOEVER, DON'T MISS!!!***
******DELIVERY ONLY******Cookies delivered still warm.
True Confections (828-350-9480)
1 Page Avenue (Grove Arcade)

Brew Pubs and Beer Joints
*Asheville Brewing Company (828-255-4077)
77 Coxe Ave.
Barley's Taproom (828-255-0504)
42 Biltmore Ave.
Bier Garden(828-285-0002)
46 Haywood St.
BoBo Gallery (828-254-3426)
22 N. Lexington Ave.
Bruisin' Ales (828-252-8999)
66 Broadway Street
Dirty Jacks (828-252-5502)
23 Buxton Ave.
*French Broad Brewing (828-277-0222)
101-D Fairview Rd.
Jack of the Wood (828-252-5445)
95 Patton Ave.
Lexington Ave. Brewery (LAB) (828-252-0212)
39 N. Lexington Ave.
Thirsty Monk (828-254-5470)
92 Patton Ave.
Wedge Brewery (828-505-2792)
125 b Roberts St., in the River Arts District

Beer City USA

Asheville narrowly edged Portland, Oregon, in the 2010 poll naming Beer City, USA. That's us, and we deserve the honor!

We'll start with **The Wedge Brewery**, arguably churning out Asheville's finest craft beer and ale (so-voted in the 2010 *Mountain Xpress* Reader's Poll.) The Wedge is located at 125b Roberts St. in the River Arts District. Their original small tasting room has surged onto the covered porch and patio, where live music brightens many an evening, and outdoor films are shown through the summer months. Open at 4 p.m. M-Th, 3 p.m. F, and 2 p.m. Sat. and Sun. Open until 10 p.m. or so, depending. Don't miss their Iron Rail IPA!

The **French Broad Tasting Room** (828-277-0222). From downtown, take Biltmore Avenue south to Biltmore Village. Turn left at McDonald's onto Lodge Street. Take the second left onto Fairview Road before the BP station. Cross the railroad tracks and look for the first building on the right. There will be signs on the building.

With paneling, a brass chandelier, candelabras and a cozy couch, the French Broad has spruced up the traditional, bare bones tasting room. The plastic cups seem out of place, but the friendly, neighborhood ambiance is appreciable in this intimate setting. There are 5 beers on tap. I like their 13 Rebels ESB.

Hours: Thursday 4 - 8 p.m. Open mic night: Friday 4 - 8 p.m.

Music at the Broad: Saturday 1 - 5 p.m.

Tours of the brewery are Saturdays at noon, 1 and 2 p.m. for $5.00.

Next up is **Dirty Jack's** (828-252- 5502) at 23 Buxton Avenue just a few miles away, but there's a lot of quick turns so pay attention.

From the French Broad Tasting Room parking lot, take a left onto Fairview Road and then a right onto Lodge Street/Sweeten Creek Road. Turn right on Biltmore Avenue. Continue on past the hospitals and turn left onto Southside Avenue. Immediately turn right onto Lexington and another immediate left on Buxton. Dirty Jack's is on the right with Green Man Brewing Company stenciled on the window.

The decor is definitely Spartan, but you're here for the beer right? Organic Green Man Ale in pint glasses are available and the ESB continues to be my all-time favorite. Three bucks buys a sampler —a taste of the four selections that happen to be on tap at the time. There's room for a couple of tables out on the sidewalk and there's two T.V.s behind the bar. Hours: Monday through Friday 4- 9 p.m.

(If the tasting rooms aren't your cup of tea (er, mug of ale?), you can find the Green Man Ale over at Jack of the Wood pub, 95 Patton Avenue (828-252-5445).)

Barley's Tap Room, downtown at 42 Biltmore Avenue, is Asheville's oldest microbrew pub. Exiting Dirty Jack's, go left on Buxton, hang a right onto South Lexington Avenue and take an immediate left on Southside Ave. Turn left on Biltmore and Barley's is about three blocks up the street on the right.

With over 46 beers on tap, one could get very distracted, but keep in mind that the purpose of the prowl is to introduce you to brews made right here in Asheville. Stick with me on this. However, the food at Barley's is great if you're hungry. (see p. 63)

Walk north on Biltmore to Patton and turn left (or if you're driving, continue another block to College St. and turn left). Continue past Pritchard Park to the intersection where College converges with Patton, at the corner of Coxe Ave. On your left, in the purple building, is the **Thirsty Monk** with two floors of excellent beer. Upstairs, fronting on Patton, they serve domestic boutique brews while the downstairs bar, facing Commerce St., offers strictly Belgian beers and ales.

From Thirsty Monk, simply stagger downhill a few blocks past the U.S. Post Office and the downtown bus station to the **Asheville Brewing Company** tasting room at 77 Coxe Avenue (828-255-4077). Brewmeister Doug Riley has come up with Shiva IPA which is their most popular beer while the Rook Porter is a rich, dark ale with a chocolaty finish. Scout Stout guarantees a "dark bark with no bite." Although it started out as a tasting room, it has grown into a full fledged pub and is a locus of progressive political partying, hosting Drinking Liberally every Thursday night and multiple other confabs and plottings.

Hours M-F from 4 p.m. "until," and Saturday and Sunday from noon, with brewery tours every Saturday.

Another half block south, Coxe intersects Hilliard. Turn right to find **Craggie Brewing** at 137 Hilliard, celebrating one year of fine brewing at this writing with an English style rye ale, an 1840s style American Ale and a Bavarian Zwickel beer as headliners. Wed.-Thurs.:4-9pm.Fri.-Sat.:4-10pm. Sunday: 2-8pm.

The **Lexington Ave. Brewery (LAB),** located at 39 N. Lexington, (828-252-0212) is a relative newcomer, but has made a notable splash in beer circles. Brewer Ben Pierson has created a tasty line up of unfiltered, naturally carbonated, additive free beers in the in-house brewery.

Outside of town, but well worth the drive and clearly part of the Asheville Beer City Movement, visit **Pisgah Brewing**, makers of certified organic beer, 150 Eastside Dr. Black Mountain, NC 28711 . (828-669-0190). Sun.2-9 p.m. Mon.-Wed.,4-9 p.m. Thurs.-at.2-12 p.m. (generally).Tours Saturday @ 2 and 3 p.m. Brews include: Nitro Stout, Pale Ale, Porter, Solstice, Cosmos, IPA, Baptista Noel, Hellbender Barleywine, Endless Summer Ale, Solstice Tripel, Apple Jaxx. Their brews are widely available at bars and restaurants in Asheville, as well.

Brew to go?

Bruisin' Ales (828-252-8999) 66 Broadway

Over 700 brews for sale. Voted #2 beer retailer in the world in 2008. If they ain't got it, you probably have to brew it yourself.

Of course, many of the breweries will sell growlers to go, and a few bottle their beers. **Highland Brewing** is the breakout leader among locals, and now distrbutes its several brews throughout the southeast U.S.

Great Smokies Craft Brewers Brewgrass Festival

Every October, Asheville hosts this variant on Oktoberfest, featuring microbrews from around the region. The festival includes a great lineup of national and regional bluegrass musicians. www.brewgrassfestival.com

Tattoos for you

Now that you're comfortably numb (see Pub Prowl on preceding pages), you may be ready for some skin art. (I personally can't imagine installing permanent pigment beneath my skin, but maybe I lack imagination.)

California Emporium of Tattoos (828-254-1747)
872 Haywood Rd. (West Asheville)
Empire Tattoo (828-252-8282)
83 Patton Avenue
Forever Tattoo (828-236-1681)
98 North Lexington Ave.
Freaks and Geeks Tattoo Sideshow (828-254-4429)
745 Haywood Rd. (West Asheville)
Hot Stuff Tattoo (828-251-6040)
428 Haywood Rd.
Liquid Dragon (828-232-2967)
66 N Lexington Avenue
Man's Ruin Tattoo (828-253-6660)
857 Merrimon Avenue (a couple of miles north of downtown, but a consistent favorite in local reader polls)

Smoke Shops

Instant Karma (828-285-899)
78 N. Lexington Ave.
Octopus Gardens (828-254-4980)
80 N. Lexington Ave.
Wonderland (828-225-5035)
33 Patton Ave.

Antiques for the rest of you

(Just guessing that the tattoo and smoke and antique crowds don't much overlap.)
N. Lexington Ave. -several shops (see map p. 23)
Broadway Ave. (see same map)
Church St. (just around the corner from Pritchard Park
Biltmore Antique District – (see map of Biltmore Ave. p. 26) , continue south on Biltmore to Riverside Dr., turn left, two blocks on left come to Antique Tobacco Barn, start there and continue east on Riverside to find more shops and directions to several others.)

Forever on the Verge—the music scene
by Steve Shanafelt and Cecil Bothwell

Music grows everywhere here. This region has long been possessed of a deep, wide pool of extremely talented and eclectic musicians, and the enthusiastic and supportive crowds have helped bring acts through the area that would normally limit themselves to much larger markets. Musicians, it seems, simply love playing Asheville.

But it wasn't always that way. In fact, following the erosion of Asheville's African-American music scene back in the 1970s, the city experience something of a live music freeze. Thanks to decades of effort by local venues and performers, the live-music loving community began to thaw out in the 1980s, and these days there's constant a supply of outstanding music on even a slow week. And thanks to large-scale events like Bele Chere, MoogFest and the Christmas Jam, national-level performers are regularly found mixing with local talent.

Granted, in recent years our music scene has seen its fair share of hype. While a few nationally touring acts do call the city home -- particularly in the acoustic singer/songwriter community -- many local musicians are content to play the occasional gig at their favorite local venue. In fact, many staggeringly skilled performers seem content to simply live in a community with other talented folks, rather than chasing the dream of financial or critical success. The upshot of this is that even a casual music listener can find outstanding performances at even the most humble local venues.

Local musicians
In recent years the Asheville area has been home to, or home-away-from-home of numerous musicians with a national or international reach: Chuck Brodsky, Tyler Ramsey, Sherri Lynn Clark, River Guergarian, Byron Hedgepeth, Warren Haynes, Stephen Heller, Malcolm Holcombe, David Holt, Billy Jonas, Christine Kane, Kellin Watson, Cactus (aka Secret Agent 23 Skidoo), Josh Lamkin, David LaMotte, Stephanie Morgan, Ozzie Orengo, Dana and Susan Robinson, Chris Rosser, Frank Southcorvo, Eliot Wadopian and David Wilcox. It would be nearly impossible to note all of the current nationally and regionally known groups from the Asheville area, but that list would include include: stephaniesid, the Stereofidelics, the Reigning Sound, GFE, Ahleuchatistas, Kings of Prussia, Hellblinki, Mad Tea Party, Sons of Ralph, Yo Mama's Big Fat Booty Band, the Steep Canyon Rangers, Menage, the Secret B-Sides and Josh Phillips Folk Festival.

Free Music

Asheville is chock-full of music. It leaks out everywhere. In fair weather you will find guitar pickers, fiddlers, horn players and even an occasional accordionist on street corners and park benches. Don't hesitate to contribute a tip to these buskers, it is our best hope of keeping them on the street. See Free listing page 48.

Asheville Civic Center (259-5544)

Haywood Street

The ACC does what civic centers do. Big name entertainers, the Asheville Symphony, Phish, Widespread Panic, Elton John, Leon Russell, Bob Dylan, sports, trade shows, high school graduations, and all the rest. At the intersection of Haywood Street, Flint Street and Page Avenue.

Barley's Tap Room (255-0504)

42 Biltmore Avenue

Easily one of Asheville's busiest venues, Barley's is very nearly a victim of its own success. Although they regularly book some of the area's best rock, country and bluegrass acts, seeing a show at here can be frustrating, as many patrons view the live music as little more than a distraction from their conversations, and talk all the more loudly to compensate. The upstairs game room and bar is a welcome haven for those seeking a less noisy night out. Barley's never charges for admission, which tends to make up for the venue's failings. Most shows start by 10pm.

www.barleystaproom.com/asheville

BoBo Gallery (254-3426)

22 Lexington Ave.

Although posing as an art gallery, Bo Bo leads a double-life as a part-time bar and trance-friendly DJ venue. The space suffers from something of an identity crisis, actually. The beer and wine bar, although suitably stiff for a gallery opening, is hardly the easiest place to kick-back and relax, and the galley itself is too small for a heated dance party. In other words, it's a great place to stand around looking hip.

Broadway's (285-0400)

113 Broadway

While first and foremost a locals-oriented bar and club, Broadway's occasionally plays a lesser role as one of Asheville's least commercial music venues. Local and regional rock bands dominate the bar's schedule, typically playing to a college-age to Gen-X crowd. While both the booking and overall quality of the shows tends to be erratic, the enthusiasm and energy of the crowd can make seeing a show at Broadway's a memorable experience. The downstairs bar and game-room is a welcome escape from the occasional bad show, and the upstairs deck is a great place to catch some fresh air during a crowded performance. Shows tend to range from $3-$10. Of all the downtown clubs, Broadway's is one of the most stringent when it comes to enforcing their sign-in policy, so come prepared to pay for a membership.

Tallgary's Pub (232-0809)
4 College Street

As one of the few downtown venues that regularly hosts cover bands as well as original acts, Tallgary's (formerly College Street Pub) has found a comfortable niche for itself in the Asheville music scene. An excellent game room, outdoor seating and decent menu go a long way towards making this venue one of Asheville's better values, although the noisy, and occasionally unruly, crowds can present a problem for a true lover of live music. Cover charges tend to be in the $2 to $7 range, and most shows start by 11pm.

Diana Wortham Theater (257-4530)
2 South Pack Square

The Diana Wortham is housed within Pack Place and is host to major productions: theater, dance, music.

Emerald Lounge (828-232-4372)
112 North Lexington Ave.

Groove, hip-hop and jam band music have found an unlikely fusion in Asheville, and no place caters to this trend better. Acts tend to be hip-hop, funk and groove performers on the fringe of the nationally-touring mainstream, as well as a healthy variety of local talent. While most shows are aimed at a dance-loving, college-age crowd, a wide variety of personalities and ages can be found strutting their stuff at the Lounge. Most shows don't begin until 11pm or later, so plan for a late night.

Firestorm Cafe (828-255-8115)
48 Commerce St.

Find a wide variety of new music and spoken word performance in this intimate space which triples as bookstore, cafe and event venue. A collective runs the place with a high level of community consciousness. Covers are low, or pay what you can. I've heard some superb performances in this, one of the newest and most progressive of Asheville's artistic endeavors.

Grey Eagle Tavern & Music Hall (828-232-5800)
185 Clingman Ave.

A quick look at the Grey Eagle's photo wall says a lot about why this low-key venue has become Asheville's favorite listening room. Big names like T-Model Ford, Arlo Guthrie, Greg Brown, Patty Larkin, Chris Smither and Leo Kottke have played intimate shows to attentive crowds here, while lesser-known acts typically find an equally receptive crowd. The Eagle is also home to an active community of local performers, making it an excellent place to play music, as well as hear it. No venue in Asheville has a better sound system and any musician who cares about sound would do well to instruct a booking agent to include the Eagle on a southeastern tour.

In keeping with the listener friendly atmosphere, most shows at the Eagle are all-ages, and many are family-friendly. Show prices can vary greatly, but most are within the $7-$15 range. Tuesdays are open mic nights, with free admission.
www.greyeaglemusic.com.

Hairspray Dance Bar & Cabaret (258-2027)
38 North French Broad Ave.

Asheville's primary presenter of drag shows, glitzy and glamorous. Probably offers the most diverse entertainment of any establishment in town. Folk to hip-hop to musical theater to rock.

Jack of the Wood (828-252-5445)
95 Patton Ave.

One of Asheville's friendliest venues, Jack of the Wood is the best place in town to catch a smoke-free night of old-time acoustic jamming and beer-fueled bluegrass sounds. Modeled on traditional Irish pubs, Jack's also has one of the most loyal crowds in Asheville. Some come for the music, but many more come for their trademark organic Green Man Ale microbrews. Their hearty pub grub is also worth sampling. Check out the Monday night Quizzo (a trivia game open to the public), the Wednesday night open old time jam, the Thursday night bluegrass jam, and the Sunday evening open Irish music session. The occasional cover charge tends to be in the $5-$10 range, and most shows start by 10pm.
www.jackofthewood.com.

Karmasonics Music & Video (828-259-9949)
19 Biltmore Avenue

New and used CDs, DVDs, live local music on third Fridays. Possibly situated atop the Giant Crystal Under the City.

Malaprop's Books and Café (828-254-6734)
55 Haywood St.
Live music some weekend nights, author events often. See more under book sellers pg.84.

Mo' Daddy's (828-258-1550)
77 Biltmore Ave.
Relative newcomer in town, with a great range of mostly local rock, blues and singer/songwriter, showcasing some of the best of Asheville's rising stars. Free to low cover.

Orange Peel Social Aid and Pleasure Club (828-225-5851)
101 Biltmore Ave.
While typically playing host to mid-level national acts, the Peel occasionally scores a knock-out headliner, even drawing international legends such as Bob Dylan, King Crimson and a two-week-long gig by Smashing Pumpkins. Ticket prices vary, but tend to be in the $10-$30 range. The Orange Peel also has a strictly enforced no-minors (18+) admission policy, so leave the kids at home.
Come prepared to stand, as seating is generally limited. www.theorangepeel.net.

Rocket Club (828-505-2494)
401 Haywood Road (West Asheville)
Opened in 2007 after lengthy delays and false-starts, including an opening night comedy extravaganza that was widely advertised and cancelled, this club proved worth the wait. The Rocket has a state-of-the art sound system, affordable drinks and "no attitude!" Open seven days with live shows Thursday through Saturday nights and the Asheville Jazz Orchestra on stage most Mondays.
www.therocketclub.net

Stella Blue (828-236-2424)
31 Patton Ave.
There's a certain smoke and shadows charm to Stella Blue. Part eclectic rock venue, part full-service bar and part pool room, Stella Blue typically serves a groove-addicted crowd who like their music with a healthy dose of noisy socialization. That said, Stella has had its share of booking coups, scoring early shows by bands like the White Stripes, Mofro, Antigone Rising and The Von Bondies. While there are occasional exceptions, Stella Blue maintains a strict no-minors admittance policy (21+). Show prices vary, but tend to be in the $7-$15 range. Seating is limited. www.stellabluelive.com.

Stella's (828-236-2424)
55 College St.

Located in the basement underneath Stella Blue, this nightspot has quickly gained a reputation for being one of the best local-music listening rooms in downtown. With ample seating, a smallish bar and a small, ground-level stage, Stella's is an intimate venue which is ideal for acts that are just getting started. Stella's is also one of the few DJ-friendly venues in town, and has regular dance events each week. Shows tend to range from $2 to $7, with most shows starting around 11pm. Stella's is a club, so memberships are required. Smoking allowed.

Tressa's Downtown Blues & Jazz (828-254-7072)
28 Broadway

As one of the few places in Asheville to be "seen," Tressa's is a place patrons either love or hate. On one hand, the club is one of the few venues in the region that actively support the small downtown jazz, blues and soul scene, and their shows tend to be among the most professional of the smaller area clubs. The crowds also tend to be very receptive and dance like there's no tomorrow. On the other hand, compared to many of the other local venues, Tressa's is expensive and less welcoming of casual music listeners.

Cover charges vary greatly, but tend to be in the $5-$15 range. www.tressas.com.

Westville Pub (828-225-9782)
777 Haywood Road (West Asheville)

As one of the few venues in West Asheville, the folks at the Westville Pub could probably get away with a mediocre music schedule and still count on a fair weekend crowd. Thankfully,

Westville goes above and beyond that expectation, and books some of the region's best rock, alternative country and roots performers.

Arrive early and take a booth for the best of both worlds. The attached game room and lounge is a little to close to the action to sneak away from a loud show for a little quiet conversation, but the small outdoor patio is a talkers (and smoker's) haven. Get to know the regulars by dropping by for a Monday night open mic, or on Tuesday for their regular blues jam.

It's also worth noting that, in an effort to remain a locals-friendly neighborhood bar, the Westville Pub never books live music or charges a cover on Friday nights. Cover prices vary, but tend to be in the $5 to $10 range.
www.westvillepub.com.

Being out in Asheville

As Alfred Kinsey established 50 years ago (and as his film bio reminded us more recently), gender lines are iffy at best. (Some would argue they are best when iffy.) And the gender preferences of clubs and bars are probably even iffier. Mostly, like most shop keepers, club owners prefer civilized customers who spend money and don't break things. Having partied at gay/lesbian clubs occasionally since the 1970s, it is my view that they are far more people-friendly and less judgmental than most sports bars—but there we run into sports preferences, a potentially lethal minefield.

The following venues are generally recognized in the community as non-gender-preference-impaired. Enjoy.

Club Hairspray (258-2027)
38 N. French Broad Avenue
Probably the most gender-optional venue in town. Home base for the Asheville Drag Queens. Indie folk, rock, poetry, dance, drama—open seven days. "Where cultures come together to play."
<www.clubhairspray.com>

O.Henry's (828-254-1891)
237 Haywood Street
Gay-friendly since 1976. Food, bar, fun. Rotating ensemble of female impersonators, weekly pool tournament. "The oldest gay bar in North Carolina!"

Scandals (828-252-2838)
11 Grove Street
Three dance floors, high energy environment, members and guests. Considered entirely friendly to asexual, bisexual, trisexual, quadrasexual ... get up and dance, dammit. "Serving our community for over 23 years."

Smokey's After Dark (828-253-2155)
18 Broadway
A long-standing very local hang-out, generally considered sort of down-scale in the old days, lately reborn as a gay bar. Could be seen as coming out of the closet late in life.

Tressa's Downtown Jazz & Blues (828-254-7072)
28 Broadway
Known for years as a lesbian bar, Tressa's is much more focussed on being the heart of Asheville's jazz scene these days.(See music listings p. 77.) But still, unquestionably, non-gender-preference-impaired.

Theater

Altamont Theatre Company (828.274.8070)
18 Church St.
Bringing NY off-Broadway performances to an intimate black-box theater space since 2010. www.myaltamont.com

Asheville Community Theatre or ACT (828-254-1320)
35 East Walnut St.
Putting on superb productions of comedy, musicals and drama since 1946. www.ashevilletheatre.org

Diana Wortham Theatre in Pack Place (828-257-4530)
2 S. Pack Square
Features national touring dance, music, off-broadway theater performances throughout the year. www.dwtheatre.com

Flat Rock Playhouse (866-732-8008)
2661 Greenville Highway, Flat Rock, NC
Since 1952. The Playhouse offers a ten-show professional series; a college apprentice and intern program; performances by the YouTheatre; year-round classes and workshops.
www.flatrockplayhouse.org

Licklog Players (828-389-8632)
In Hayesville, N.C. Covers a five county area in North Georgia and Western North Carolina. Each season, Licklog Players produces a full slate of musicals, comedies, and dramas in its Peacock Theatre.
www.licklogplayers.org

NC Stage Company (828-669-4367) 33 Haywood Street
Asheville's professional and often experimental theatre. Voted Asheville's Best Local Theater for three years in a row for a diverse season of gripping dramas, classics, family plays and comedies.
www.ncstage.org

Montford Park Players (828-254-5116)
An all volunteer troupe presenting their love of Shakespeare to friends and neighbors. Also presents Dickens' "A Christmas Carol" each December. www.montfordparkplayers.org

Southern Appalachian Repertory Theatre or SART
(828-689-1384) 44 College Street, Mars Hill, NC
Presents plays concerning Appalachia that portray the rich culture and heritage of our region.
www.sartheatre.com

Literary Matters

Asheville has a glittering literary history peopled by writers of staggering reputation. As I wrote in a book review for *Mountain Xpress*:

"Staggering" is sometimes too apt—and probably no more so than for F. Scott Fitzgerald, who in the 1930s roared through these parts on the bedraggled coattails of the Jazz Age, fueled by beer, bourbon, gin and champagne, and leaving behind a wife, plus a trail of empties, debts and rumors of bacchanalian affairs.

In many ways, the image that Fitzgerald cultivated throughout his brief life and more briefly brilliant career is perfectly suited to a high-end hostelry. Glamour out the wazoo, tête-à-têtes with Hollywood auteurs, expatriate flamboyance and steamships plying the Atlantic, witty conversation and cocktail hours that stretched from the forenoon past midnight—exotic, expensive and flirting with danger. In the public mind, Fitzgerald was Gatsby.

What more can a grand hotel require of a guest?

After installing his wife, Zelda, in nearby Highland Hospital in Montford—where she remained until a fire killed her in 1948—Fitzgerald, who came to Asheville ostensibly to revive his own failing health, spent two gin-soaked summers at the Grove Park Inn. While living there in 1935 and 1936, he allegedly pursued a tryst with a Texas socialite, drank, tried to write, drank, attempted suicide, drank, and then drank some more. It is fitting, therefore, that GPI holds an annual event—A Salute to F. Scott Fitzgerald—on the writer's birthday weekend (he was born Sept. 24, 1896), the better to inflame fans and distill the sour mash of his memory.

Then, too, we had Thomas Wolfe, whose boyhood home is a downtown museum (restored after an arson's fire ate much of the building in 1998). On the edge of town there is a log cabin where Wolfe spent a few months when he returned after publication of *Look Homeward, Angel*, and where he did his only writing in these parts. (Wolfe was actually a New York literary figure in his day.) His abbreviated stint in Asheville was reportedly sodden as well, though not as flamboyantly as Fitzgerald's. We claim him anyway.

As for the semi-autobiographical *Angel*, a goodly portion of the town's citizenry were purportedly outraged by Wolfe's loose lips concerning family and neighbors. If so, folks in those high and far off times must have had a low boredom quotient. In twenty-five years living in Buncombe County I have only met two people who admitted to actually reading the whole book. One of those, Steve, a co-author of this volume, had to escape to Central America and hole up out of reach of modern culture to work through it.

Steve: *No one ever reads Thomas Wolfe's* Look Homeward, Angel *for fun. In fact, the only way it ever gets read is if there's absolutely nothing else to do, or if there's a lot of money involved. Let's face it; the book is a bore. It's a beautiful, elegant, soul consuming bore, but it's a bore nonetheless.*

Reading Look Homeward, Angel *is almost exactly like being on a date with a very attractive, well-educated, spiritually enlightened girl who annoyingly turns every topic of conversation into some rambling anecdote from her past. These may, or may not, have thing one to do with whatever it was you were wanting to talk about, but she doesn't seem to care all that much. She just talks. On and on. After a while, most readers start looking around for the waiter to bring them the check.*

In that vein, the good thing about Thomas Wolfe's writing is this; if you can make it through dinner and the chatty cab ride back to her place, you will be rewarded with some of the most mind-blowing literary dirty talk and finger-to-page sex you've ever had. It's truly astounding stuff.

And why is it so good? Because the girl ... I mean book ... really makes you work for it. Each brilliantly buried description is like that first time you brush hands. The first truly moving passage, that achingly desired first kiss, is buried more than a hundred pages in. By the time you figure out where the story is finally going, and you've slipped under the sheets and skin starts meeting skin, you've waded through tens of thousands of words.

But when you get there, when you've finally made it to the sticky, wet ending of the tale, you'll see why Wolfe is a legend. A stuck-up, hard-to-get, self-absorbed legend that is more high-maintenance than a Manhattan socialite, but a legend nonetheless.

Another friend who had to read it for school, "read the Cliff's Notes."

Ink must have been cheaper in those days, too. Every writer in my acquaintance who has attempted the density of *Angel* says "he needed an editor," notwithstanding the fact that Wolfe did have an editor who lopped off about half of the original text. I made it through about three chapters and belatedly remembered that I had a coffee can full of pennies that wanted rolling, house plants to water and drawers that hadn't been organized since I built my house in 1981. I suppose I discovered I couldn't go *Homeward* again, or, to go with Steve's metaphor, I never asked for another date.

In any event, the tourism folks make great hay of his notoriety, in the same vein as a "Shootout at the O.K. Corrall," or "The world's biggest ball of string," works for other locales. Wolfe is buried in Riverside Cemetery.

To wit: Asheville hosts the annual Thomas Wolfe Festival, a four day event centered on the dude's Oct. 3 birthday

O. Henry is also buried in Riverside Cemetery, an appropriately surprise ending—since he never resided here. Though he hailed from Greensboro, North Carolina, O. Henry much preferred west Texas. While resident there he was found guilty of embezzlement and spent time in a federal penitentiary in Ohio where he honed his writing skill. Post prison he drifted to New York City where he fell prey to alcoholism, influenza and diabetes. Dead at 48 of cirrhosis of the liver, his second wife (a Weaverville native) brought him home for interment.

In the Modern Era, it would be difficult for any native scribbler to top Asheville-born Charles Frazier, whose splendid novel-turned-movie *Cold Mountain* was his literary debut. Nice start, Charlie! His second foray, *Thirteen Moons,* is also superb.

In 2004 West Asheville-based poet and educator Allan Wolf published the most engaging and readable account of the Lewis and Clark Expedition amongst a torrent of related titles in the expedition's bicentennial era. *New Found Land* was penned for young adult readers, but impressed the hell out of me. Read it. Wolf's children's poetry volume *The Blood-Hungry Spleen and Other Poems About Our Parts* is wonderful as well, arguably the best read-aloud about anatomy in or out of print.

Poet Glenis Redmond has primarily built her reputation on live performance, but has published *Backbone*, *Glenis on Poetry* (cd) and *Mama's Magic Video* (VHS).

Poet, essayist and playwright David Brendan Hopes has turned out six books, the latest *A Dream of Adonis*. In addition, he's penned several plays including *The Christmas Count* and *The Book of the Mystic*, both of which made it to Broadway. Go Dave!

Novelist, historian and Beaverdam native Wilma Dykeman is author of 16 books and a Guggenheim Fellow and winner of many literary recognitions and awards. *The Tall Woman* is probably Dykeman's most popular and best-loved novel. Dykeman's *The French Broad* is widely touted as a grand history of our river and Asheville, but I find it tedious and overblown and overweening in its praise of her family business (Stokely foods).

Nan Chase delivered the best overview of this city in her 2007 book, *Asheville: A History*. As I wrote in a review of the book:

This is a fine example of critical history, the result of an investigation below the surface aimed at explanation of how the modern city came to be and where it might be headed. Chase writes, "Because many of my interviews were leading me to wonder about Asheville's future I decided to extend this story as well, to include the hopes and fears of various Asheville activists for the next decade or two and to see how close reality comes."

Contemporary novelist Gail Godwin makes many allusions to her hometown in books including *Father Melancholy's Daughter*. Godwin now lives in Woodstock, New York. Woodstock is very toney.

Asheville native John Ehle, born here in 1925, wrote about this region in works such as his 1961 novel *Lion in the Hearth*.

UNCA professor Peggy Parris made a splash with the 1992 publication of her first novel *Waltzing in the Attic* and, at last report, was working on her third—a fictional autobiography of the English suffragette, Lady Constance Lytton. Her deep commitment to local literary endeavor continues. Yo Peggy! You rock.

Warren Wilson College, a little way east of Asheville offers one of only two creative writing graduate programs in the United States and features frequent lectures and readings by prominent contemporary authors.

If you are intrigued by local writers, check out *Scribblers: Stalking the Authors of Appalachia* by Stephen Kirk, a wonderful collection of WNC gossip and fact about the writers who have called this place home—or slept here, at any rate.

Black Mountain College

Avant-garde writers, artists and poets from all over the world flocked to Black Mountain College during the 1930s and 1940s. Although it was active for less than three decades, this innovative education center nurtured original ideas and altruism. Josef Albers, John Dewey, Albert Einstein, Buckminster Fuller, Henry Miller and Thornton Wilder are just a few of the great intellectuals who visited and lectured at Black Mountain. Bucky built his first geodesic dome here. As Thornton would say, "All are sleeping, sleeping on the hill." Visit the Black Mountain College Museum to learn more (p. 56).

Book Sellers

Ah, bookstores. What would we do without them?

Asheville is graced with a handful of independent book sellers,. the only kind we recommend. Sadly that number has dwindled since the first edition of this guide book. We've lost one new and two used booksellers since 2005. The big chains have become so powerful that they are able to dictate content to publishers. What occurs is censorship—unseen, rarely reported, but very real.

Avoid chain bookstores. And if you shop online, try using Booksense.com (the indy Web source) instead of Amazon.

On the flip side, it would be disingenuous to ignore the fact that Amazon.com has been the second-largest sales venue for *Finding your way in Asheville*, after Malaprop's Books and Cafe. It has enabled Brave Ulysses Books, a very tiny publishing company, to sell books globally, a platform completely unavailable to small publishers in the past. Roses have thorns, and clouds, silver linings.

The Captain's Bookshelf (828-253-6631) 31Page Avenue
Specializing in rare and wonderful volumes, Captain's is where to go for a wide selection of arcana and knowledgeable help in finding or discovering your heart's desire.

Downtown Books and News (828-253-8654)
63 North Lexington Street
Best magazine selection in town, plus shelves and shelves and shelves and shelves of well organized used books maintained by a helpful staff. Plus a wonderful cat.

Firestorm Café and Books (828-255-8115)
48 Commerce Street
Progressive to radical literature in a venue operated by a 12-member collective. Host to music, conferences and lectures from the left and from the heart. Great place to meet similarly minded folk for conversation and collaboration.

*Malaprop's Books and Café (828-254-6734)
55 Haywood Street
The mother of Asheville's indies, Malaprop's is fittingly located very near the heart of the city (see Pritchard Park, p. 21). With author readings, musical and poetry performances, internet access and lots and lots of glorious books, M'prop's is legendary and great.

Spellbound Children's Bookshop (828-232-2228)
19 Wall Street
Nothing but kids' reading matter with a proprietor who loves children. Weekly read-aloud events. Spellbound is where tomorrow's Asheville readers get started.

And just out of downtown:
Accent on Books (828-252-6255) 854 Merrimon (new)
Lin Digs Books (828-236-0669) 217 Merrimon (used)
Saints & Scholars Book Company (828-251-5558) 474 Haywood Road (new)

High country low-down

North Carolina's mountain region, that is to say, WNC, has pretty much everything an outdoorsy sort could possibly wish for outside of ocean frontage. And that could be in the cards since sea level is rising due to global warming. Surfin' safari to Greenville, anyone?

Thanks to the terrain, farming and development here have historically been confined to the valleys, and even the loggers gave up when confronted by steep escarpments. So we have substantial swaths of old growth forest here, connected by vast tracts of younger trees, and every amenity that forestation provides. Abundant wildlife, clean water and scenic falls, wilderness to provide solitude, trails that range from casual walks to arduous challenges and, everywhere, beautiful vistas to buoy the spirits.

Whatever your preferred mode of enjoyment you will find friends and outfitters here who can help you dive into the green. Walk along Asheville's greenways or head off for solo backpacking in Shining Rock Wilderness. Enjoy lazy flat-water canoeing on the French Broad or thrill-a-minute rafting and kayaking in nearby gorges. Go road biking along quiet country roads or make a mad scramble through the Alexander Mountain Bike Facility. There is a way to get way into the outdoors here.

And for campers the options run from Poupon-passing cheek-to--cheek tenting at the annual Lake Eden Arts Festival, to RV sites along the Blue Ridge Parkway, to pastoral isolation down in a "holler" or "just up the branch."

A word of caution, however: ozone.

As pristine as our forests may appear, we are at the wrong end of a geographic funnel. The smokestacks of TVA coal-fired power plants and numerous industries are upwind of us here, plus the exhaust pipes of local and interstate traffic. All of that gunk blows this direction and is forced up over the mountains. The health risk is real. Pay attention to ozone warnings and do what you can to reduce the problem (conserve energy every way you know how and learn more).

Someday, we will all breathe easier.

On the other hand, as John Maynard Keynes famously observed: "In the long run we will all be dead."

Mountain Sports Festival

The Mountain Sports Festival, usually held the last weekend in May, free for spectators, fee for some events. (see Free events, p. 48)
If you are a competitor (or enjoy competition) check out the Web site. www.mountainsportsfestival.com/

Outdoor Connections

Blue Ridge Parkway (828-298-0398)
(for information about closings, weather)
www.nps.gov/blri/index.htm

Great Smoky Mountains National Park
www.nps.gov/grsm/index.htm

National Forests in North Carolina (828-257-4200)
www.cs.unca.edu/nfsnc
Asheville is surrounded by the Nantahala and Pisgah National
Forests. There are more great places to hike, canoe, camp and enjoy
the outdoors than I could fit into this book. Contact the rangers or
local outfitters for more info.

Riverside Cemetery
We included the cemetery here for lack of a better place to park it.
Riverside is a lovely tree-shaded hillside, perfect for an afternoon
walk or a bike ride. It used to go right down to the river before the
highway (now I-26) intervened. O. Henry, Thomas Wolfe, Zebulon
Vance and other notable locals are buried here.
From Pritchard Park, drive north on Haywood Street, curve past
Basilica St. Lawrence, continue to the light at Montford Avenue, turn
right, cross I-240. Continue north, turn left on Cullowhee Street,
right on Pearson Drive, left on Birch Street, continue to end.

WNC Nature Center (828-298-5600)
75 Gashes Creek Road
(See info under Family Outings, p. 42)
www.wncnaturecenter.org

Great all-around Web site for outdoor drives and hikes:
www.westernncattractions.com/Parks.htm

Take me to the river

Mountains squeeze clouds like sponges. As warm wet air is forced up and over by prevailing winds, rapid cooling causes condensation and down it comes, in buckets. The same verticality encourages rapid run-off toward flatter terrain, and, before you know it, the creek is full of people in kayaks, dodging rocks, rolling, whooping, hollering, having way too much fun and occasionally being swept to their deaths.

Any paddle sport enthusiast, from the rank beginner to Olympic contender, can find a place to happily play in easy reach from Asheville.

The author on the French Broad.

The **French Broad River** is the longest playground, with numerous take-outs along more than 25 miles of flat water from Henderson County to just above the dam in Woodfin (yes, it runs north, like the Nile). Below the dam (where there is an easy portage to the left) the whitewater begins. From tons of fun to hair-raising to life-threatening, the series of rapids and falls runs north past Hot Springs, with somewhat fewer take-outs. (A guide service or rafting company is a safe choice for first-timers.)

The **Swannanoa River** is flat and navigable for most of its length from Black Mountain to the French Broad near Amboy Road.

Further out, some stretches of the **Broad River** and **Rocky Broad** above **Lake Lure** are kayakable, and below that dam a flat water stretch extends miles toward Rutherfordton.

South of Hendersonville, the **Green River** boasts excellent whitewater runs.

The **Nantahala Gorge**, northwest of Asheville, is the most famous whitewater run in the region, and boasts stretches suitable for adept amateurs or daredevil experts as it runs west from Bryson City.

Beginning river rats should be aware that conditions vary widely by season and depending on rainfall. Yesterday's placid meander can become a raging torrent following a round of heavy thunderstorms. (This writer almost lost a paddling companion six summers back. Forty years of experience in canoes didn't mean diddly when we breached in a drop and were sucked into a whirlpool. We weren't wearing life jackets. She nearly drowned.)

Outfitters

Adventurous Fast Rivers Rafting (800-438-7238) Located on the Nantahala River 1.25 hours from Asheville. Offers guided or unguided rafting trips, fun-yaks, sit-on-top kayaks, inflatable canoes, lake canoes and kayak instruction. Reservations suggested or required depending on time of the season. www.white-water.com

Asheville Outdoors (828-669-6886) Located in Black Mountain and owned and operated by outdoor education graduates. They offer instruction and guided tours for back-packing, rock climbing and whitewater kayaking. All guides are professionally degreed and insured, implementing the highest safety standards. Please call in advance. www.ashevilleoutdoors.net

Black Dome Mountain Sports (828-251-2001)
Lots of gear for camping, hiking, backpacking, montaineering and the rest. Lots of information from well-informed staffers.

Diamond Brand Outdoors (828-251-4668) Please call in advance. Canoes and a variety of kayaks are available for rent by the day or week-end. Locations in Asheville and Arden.
www.diamondbrand.com

Headwaters Outfitters (828-877-3106) Located one hour southwest of Asheville just outside of Brevard. Headwaters has been in the canoeing, kayaking and tubing biz since 1990. Explore the scenic French Broad River with 3, 4 and 7 hour self-guided trips available. Reservations required. www.headwatersoutfitters.com

Nantahala Outdoor Center (800-232-7238) Six locations, the closest just a half hour or so north of Asheville; focussed on rafting and kayaking. In operation since 1972. Half-day, full-day and overnighter trips on the French Broad River. Reservations required. www.noc.com

Southern Waterways (800-849-1970) Canoeing, rafting or kayaking in Asheville on the quiet, scenic French Broad River through the Biltmore Estate property. Closest to downtown. www.paddlewithus.com

Wild things

Asheville is bordered by national forests and a national park, bisected by the French Broad River and connected to the rest of the Appalachian Mountain chain by a wildlife corridor known as the Blue Ridge Parkway. We have a lot of what passes for the natural world in North America in the 21st Century. There is a little bit of old-growth woodland left in places where steep terrain prevented logging operations (see "Flora" below) and while air pollution is defoliating forests on the higher peaks, second- and third-growth forests cover much of the region. This is about as good a place for critters as can be found in the contiguous 48 states. Visit the WNC Nature Center to learn more about local fauna and ecosystems.

Birds

One look at a topographic map of Eastern North America is all it takes to understand why Asheville is a birder's paradise. To the north and west there is a vast expanse of summer habitat stretching up to the edge of the Arctic ice sheets. To the south and east lie winter vacation habitats in the tidewater swamps of the Carolinas, and the bayou country along the Gulf, together with the Central Florida greenway that stretches from Georgia's Okefenokee Swamp to the Everglades. And, of course, the beaches. Plus jumping off points for the flight to Cuba, the Caribbean and South America. Betwixt the two is that long swath of ancient upland known as the Appalachians —and there aren't all that many north/south gaps in the chain.

Boy, do we get a lot of visitors. Birds too, for the same reason.

Most of the species of birds with northern ranges on this side of the continent have been spotted in the greater Asheville area at one time or another (with the exception of dedicated tropical birds that only visit coastal areas), and a wide variety stick around to raise a family. Among the regulars, none sing more sweetly than the wood thrush. If you hike in forested areas near water in the summer months you are certain to hear its flute-like melody.

If you can manage to quit jabbering while you hike in late winter and spring, you are bound to hear the drumming of the ruffed grouse. A lot of folks never hear these chicken-sized ground-dwellers because they simply can't shut up—but if you are quiet, you will hear a sound like someone trying (unsuccessfully) to start a chain saw in the next holler. THUMP, THUMP, thump, thump, thump-thump-

thump-thump. Somewhere nearby, a male bird is attracting a mate by flapping his wings, puffing his chest, fluffing his ruff and generally making a fool of himself. Similar behavior is not uncommon in downtown bars.

This region's ubiquitous dogwood trees are loaded with red berries in the fall and you can frequently spot flocks of migrating cedar waxwings clustered on the branches. Watch for their characteristic food-sharing behavior. One waxwing will pick a berry and turn to pass it to the next and on down the line like a bucket brigade. They appear to enjoy the game.

We have a rainbow of feather options to suit your birding whim. Scarlet tanagers are not uncommon in the tree tops, though they are harder to spot than you would imagine, given their brilliant coloration. Their less striking cousins, the summer tanagers, nest here as well. Purple and house finches are somewhat maroon, and very common. In the blue arena, indigo buntings are everywhere—displaying a flash of iridescence as they careen in the sunlight—and Eastern bluebirds are frequently spotted near pastures and open fields. The American goldfinch is a year-round resident and, if orange is your thing, the Northern (or Baltimore) oriole summers here as well. Rufous-sided towhees with their orange-brown side panels, are commonly discovered scratching up the leaves beneath understory shrubs in the forest as they call, "towheeee!" Greenish feathers are flapped by any number of female and juvenile birds, but none outshine the dainty ruby throated hummingbird, and this writer has occasionally seen parakeets (budgerigars)—no doubt escapees who surely headed south or expired in short order.

Asheville's pigeons are worthy of note because they provide a food supply for peregrine falcons, which nest atop office buildings. Keep an eye on rooflines downtown to spot them perching amongst the gargoyles. The falcon population, once threatened with extinction due to DDT, has rebounded since that poison was banned, and the species was reintroduced to this region in the 1990s. The "cliffs" in the city serve as well as cliffs in the gorges for falcon habitat. Other common local raptors include the American kestrel; broad-winged-Cooper's-, red-shouldered-, red-tailed-, and sharp-shinned-hawks; the northern harrier; barred, barn and screech owls; and black and turkey vultures. Golden eagles are very occasionally spotted in the winter.

Pileated woodpeckers (pictured here) are locally common. You'll hear the Woody Woodpecker laughter and heavy-duty hammering of these large, striking birds throughout our forests. Watch for their swooping flights, white underwing-bars (on jet-black) and bright red top-knots.

Wild turkeys? We got 'em. Even inside the city limits. You can spot whole flocks of these magnificent birds in large suburban yards in north Asheville and on farm acreage in every valley. When a dozen or more nearly four-foot-long birds takes off and swoops into the trees you are allowed to gasp. (For info on the bronze turkeys downtown see Urban Trail, p. 35)

No discussion of avian Asheville would be complete without mention of the chimney swifts at the Grove Arcade. Each autumn swifts gather into flocks numbering in the thousands before beginning their flight to South America. One gathering point is the giant chimney atop the Arcade. Each night, beginning in September, a spiral cloud of swifts collects above the chimney, swirling and swirling. Then,as twilight falls they begin to plummet into the chimney. One can only imagine the dense mass of birds there, all clinging to the walls and each other, upside down, to spend a chill autumn night in mutual warmth. When a major cold front nears, suddenly, they are gone—off to warmer climes. For more info, guided walks and birding gear, visit **The Compleat Naturalist** in Biltmore.

Mammals

WNC is home to all the usual urban and exurban furry friends from mice to muskrats to opossums (a marsupial, not a mammal), raccoons and white-tailed deer. But there are a few larger critters that bear particular mention, and one family of very small ones.

Black bears for one. Despite continued habitat loss due to development and a severe decline in the oak forest which provides the acorns that comprise much of their diet—plus ongoing pressure from hunters— these lumbering, gentle omnivores are still clinging to survival in the mountains. In bad times, when the  acorn crop is particularly sparse and they are faced with the urgent necessity of tanking up before hibernation, hungry bears will scavenge everywhere for food. Even in town. Nearly every year, a bear wanders into urban Asheville, Black Mountain, Hendersonville or Waynesville. In suburbia it is even more common.

Black bears are a lot more scared of you than you are of them and unless you get between a mother and her cubs there is almost no way to make one confront you, no matter what stories you may have heard. Black bear attacks are exceedingly rare. They will get into your food when you are camping, or into your compost pile or garbage can. Like any wild creature they can be unpredictable when they are frightened and cornered. Give them space. Appreciate them for the survivors they are. And if you don't want to share your food or garbage when you are camping, string it up in a tree or tuck it in a vehicle. They were here first. (In national park campgrounds this rule is firmly enforced. If you leave food around your camp site you will be ordered to leave. Immediately. Even in the middle of the night if that's when a ranger discovers your oversight.)

The biggest current threat to our bears is probably from Southeast Asia where bear gallbladders are imagined to have aphrodisiacal power. Rings of Appalachian bear poachers supplying that market have been broken up in recent years. Fortunately, Viagra and other over-the-counter nostrums have proven more effective as love potions and there has been a marked decrease in demand for animal parts—some wildlife authorities believe Viagra (et. al.) may yet save tigers, seals, rhinos and an endangered swift whose penis bones (tiger and seal), horn and nest have been weirdly credited with increasing libido in the past. Go figure.

Mountain lions live here too. The U.S. Fish and Wildlife service insists that they aren't indigenous creatures but are escaped western lions. (Some benighted idiots actually keep these magnificent cats as "pets" and they fairly frequently get loose.) The reason the USFWS wants to call them "escapees" is that IF they were native eastern cats it would be necessary to protect their habitat because they would qualify as an endangered subspecies. This is, of course, ludicrous bureaucratic hair-splitting, being done to avoid the financial and political cost of protecting our cougars. All of the mountain lions (cougars, pumas, catamounts, same difference) in North America can interbreed, so who's kidding whom about whether ours deserve protection????

Write your congressional reps.

But the main point is, they are here. One morning, just past dawn, I was driving a mountain road in southeast Buncombe County and a huge tawny cat bounded across the road in two leaps and disappeared into the rhododendrons. I won't ever forget the sight. In over two decades living in these mountains I have heard many other big cats caterwauling. The mating call is thrilling, some say "blood-curdling," and sounds very much like a woman screaming. I am not alone. Sightings are common.

In the western U.S. there are occasional attacks on humans. None have been verified in the east in many decades, but it could happen. If this possibility frightens you, don't hike alone and particularly avoid running alone in remote places. (Running stimulates the predator/prey reaction in felines. Note a house cat's differential reaction to a ball of yarn sitting still and a ball of yarn being dragged across the floor. Now multiply your cat's weight by a factor of six. You are the yarn ball.) If this scares you a lot, jog downtown.

Coyotes have moved into WNC in recent decades and their rapturous singing can be heard throughout the region, particularly when the moon is full. They seem to be far cleverer than bears when it comes to avoiding human contact and it is very unlikely that you will catch more than a fleeting glimpse as one dashes across the road. The odds of seeing one while hiking are remote.

River otters, extirpated by trappers in the 19th century, were successfully reintroduced here in the late 1980s and are gradually expand ing their range. You are most apt to see them when canoeing in flat-water stretches of the French Broad River and its tributaries.

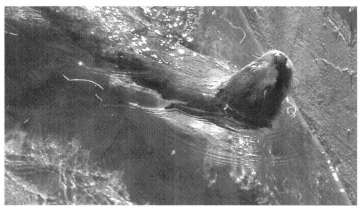

Elk have been reintroduced in these parts, after being wiped out by hunters in the mid-19th century, though they are presently only found in a limited range in the Great Smoky Mountains National Park. Check with the park office for more info on elk spotting.

Bison, once native to this region, have been raised for slaughter here for about two decades and at this writing may soon have a refuge where they will once again roam "free." The last wild buffalo hereabouts was killed at the accordingly named Bull Gap, milepost 375 on the Blue Ridge Parkway.

Bats are amazing, fascinating, irreplaceable, misunderstood and often endangered animals. In WNC we have big brown bats and little brown bats; the Indiana myotis and Keen's myotis; Eastern pipistrelles; red bats; hoary bats; evening bats; and Rafinesque's big-eared bats.

Don't you love that name?

These good buddies eat more than their weight in insects every night, and altogether consume hundreds of tons of WNC bugs each summer. They can carry rabies, but do so far more rarely than raccoons. Locally, the big buzz about bats comes from Bat Cave, a tiny town named for, you got it, a bat cave located there. The Nature Conservancy leads tours to the cave in the summer. Unescorted visits are forbidden because a certain subset of yahoos with more air than neurons between their ears decided that exploding fireworks in the cave was enormous fun.

Reptiles and Amphibians

Frogs, toads, salamanders and snakes abound in WNC, together with a smattering of lizards and a declining turtle population. From tiny peepers and brilliant green tree frogs to bullfrogs, the wet woods in this region are home to a wide variety of species. You will chiefly hear them at dawn and dusk when their love songs fill the air. Toads join the chorus, particularly during the spring mating season. Sometimes taken for granted, amphibians represent the largest portion of protoplasm in most temperate woodlands and toads can live to 30 years of age. If you don't like mosquitoes, you should consider frogs and toads to be buddies nearly on a par with bats, if somewhat less cuddly.

A particularly unusual phenomena occurs in late-winter in this region, following some warm days and rain in March (though this writer has witnessed it in February one year). Frogs by the tens of thousands will head out looking for mates. You will see hundreds on particular stretches of road at night, many run over, of course, and the night air reeks from the carnage. If you are out for a stroll at dawn the next day you will spy raccoons, possums and free range chickens in the neighborhood cleaning up the leftovers.

These mountains are home to an equally diverse population of salamanders, some rare or endangered, though you are unlikely to see many unless you make a dedicated effort.

Snakes get unwarranted attention, probably due to some kind of genetic memory that goes all the way back to our monkey days. Sure, there are a few poisonous ones eking out a living, but the vast majority here are entirely harmless.

The most commonly seen serpent in this region is probably the black rat snake. Rat snakes are constrictors, meaning that they kill their prey by grabbing it, encircling it and gradually tightening coils until inhalation ceases. They eat rodents, birds and other snakes. These guys may exceed six feet when full grown, though I have only seen one that big during twenty-five years living and hiking in these mountains. Adults are black with a grey stomach. Juveniles are blotched, with squarish dark spots on a grey background. No black snake in North America is poisonous.

Next in order of sightings is the Northern water snake, commonly found, you guessed it, in or near water. Food consists of frogs and fish which are swallowed alive. They may rarely reach 50 inches in length, vary in color from greenish to dark grey to brownish, and are banded when young, becoming darker and more solid as they age.

No aquatic snake in our region is poisonous (though any snake can swim in a pinch).

The familiar common garter snake is the most widely distributed snake in North America. Diet is bugs and occasional small mice, lizards or birds. They may exceed four feet in length, and here, like everywhere else, they are striped with yellow from head to tail, interspersed with brownish, greenish or sometimes bluish stripes.

No vertically striped snake in North America is poisonous.

In this writer's experience, the next most commonly sighted snake is the diminutive Northern ring-necked snake. These shy little animals subsist on earthworms, slugs, lizards and newborn snakes. I've never seen one more than two feet in length, and rarely above one foot. They are solid dusky grey-brown to black with a cream colored neck ring and a brilliant orange stomach.

No snake in North America with a single neck ring is poisonous.

You may encounter a dozen or so other non-poisonous species if you spend enough time outdoors here and I heartily recommend the Audubon Society Field Guide to North American Reptiles and Amphibians if you want to learn to identify them all. All of the nonpoisonous snakes in our region have round pupils, whereas the two poisonous species' pupils are vertical "cats" eyes (for the same reason as felines—they are nocturnal). This difference is much easier to see at a distance than you may imagine.

No snake with round pupils in our region is poisonous.

There are only two poisonous species in WNC. The copperhead is the more common of the two. Copperheads are very distinctively colored, with a flat somewhat triangular head the color of a dull or dusty new penny and alternating "cigar" bands of pale beige or grey and darker brown, all the way down the body. This and the timber rattler are the only snakes in our region with such "cigar" banding and once you see them you will never mistake them for anything else. (Visit the WNC Nature Center.)

The copperhead is a shy and totally unaggressive snake. I have worked around them in a garden while they stayed absolutely still, depending on their camouflage coloration for security. I have moved flower pots in which they were curled (unknown to me) after which they slid out and skidded away as quickly as possible. I have picked them up to relocate them from neighbors' yards and have never had one even attempt to bite me. **Yes, they are poisonous, but there is no recorded death of a human due to a copperhead bite.**

Ever.

Anywhere.

Zilch.

No matter what crazy stories you hear. None. **Nada.**

A victim will get an infection, possibly lose some flesh and occasionally suffer other serious but temporary repercussions. You could lose a digit to gangrene, particularly if treatment is much delayed. If you are bitten, seek medical help ASAP but don't freak out. You are going to be okay.

Then we have the timber rattlesnake. Like the copperhead, the color pattern is banded, although the rattler's bands may be broken up a bit. There is a similar, darker version of this snake in the northeast, but ours are yellowish-, brownish- or pinkish-grey with a tan or reddish-brown back stripe dividing chevron-like cross-bands. The cross-bands are dark brown to black and edged with cream or yellow. The effect is as distinctly banded as the copperhead and the tail is black. This is a heavy-bodied snake and the neck is distinctly slimmer than the somewhat triangular head or thick body. Usually there are rattles on the tail (though they break off and may not be present). Many snake species vibrate their tails when disturbed, and rattlers get their name from the distinctive buzz generated by their unique tail ornament.

These guys are more serious. They are much more likely to stand their ground (reports of ANY North American snake chasing a human are exaggerations and lies and fabrications and bull-dinky), and they are apt to strike if they feel threatened. (The first strike is often with mouth closed—to scare off the intruder. You see, snake's poison is only available in a limited quantity and it takes the snake's body time to produce more. So if a venomous snake wastes it's load unnecessarily it ends up like the gunman in a movie thriller with an empty clip. Snakes hardly have what you would call a brain, they are really just a bundle of reflexes, so they don't reason this out. But over the aeons they have developed a propensity not to empty their clips on a whim.)

If you are bitten it may be fatal, though deaths are rare. Seek help ASAP. It is best to keep your heart rate low to slow spread of the poison. If you have far to go, a snug but not tight tourniquet can help isolate the poison. Cutting the fang marks and sucking out the poison is generally not advised these days unless you are a LONG, LONG way from help. Bites are usually on a hand or leg, so elevate the limb en route to medical care. Try to remain calm and repeat after me: deaths are rare.

How to not get bitten by a poisonous snake

Don't mess with them. It is a fact that most people who get bitten are attempting to catch or kill the snake that bites them. Look before you step or put your hand somewhere. Copperheads and rattlesnakes are almost exclusively nocturnal in the summer (use a flashlight and stick to paths at night). Be aware that any snake species may be out sunning on warm rocks in the spring or fall -- they are cold blooded and depend on sunlight for body heat. Both copperheads and rattlesnakes give birth—eggs are retained inside the mother rather than being laid in a warm location as with all of the other species in our region—so gravid females are particularly likely to be sunning themselves in the springtime. This is the equivalent behavior to a hen sitting on a nest. Flat, rocky, outcroppings are favorite basking locations as they tend to be tree-free due to sparse soil. Pay attention when you climb up on the rocks to enjoy the view.

All species of snake hibernate in the winter, so you are most unlikely to encounter any of these critters between November and April.

Slow and solid

Turtles are broadly divided into two categories: water and land. We have the usual run of aquatic species including the snapping, stinkpot or musk, painted and pond slider turtles in waterways and ponds. We are also home to a good number of Eastern box turtles, though their numbers are in steep decline. Box turtles were hunted to near-extinction from Ohio to New England by Native Americans who ate the meat and used the shells for ornaments and rattles. Slaughter of the animals for ornament continues today, among native wannabes who market rattles to the tourist and new-age crowd. But nowadays the greater pressure is from China which has extirpated its own turtle population and now reaches around the globe to fill aphrodisiac prescriptions. (See note about Viagra under Bears, p. 99.)

Bugs

Butterflies flit in grand abundance in this region. Because agriculture is limited to river valleys and so much of the land area is more or less wild, we haven't been doused with as many pesticides as much of the continent north or south of here. On top of that, the dizzying number of wildflowers (see "Flora" below) provides food for a myriad of species. Of particular note is the annual migration of monarch butterflies, which fly en masse from Canada and the northeast U.S. to Mexico each fall (see mural on back cover). Most of the monarchs cross these mountains in the vicinity of Tunnel Gap at milepost 415 on the Blue Ridge Parkway during the third week of September and visitors find the air and fields full of fluttering orange and black beauties.

Amongst biting bugs, we've got all the usual culprits, though fewer than many regions. Water tends to run downhill fast here, too fast to permit the extensive breeding of mosquitoes seen in swampier climes. And while we have some black flies, visitors from New England or Canada find our pitiful local swarms merely amusing.

Ticks can be a nuisance, particularly in late summer. Do a tick check of hairline, armpits, navel, crotch and under elastic band lines of underwear after late summer hikes. Lyme disease is less prevalent here than in the Northeast, but it is around. Touching the butt end of a tick with a hot extinguished match usually makes it back out. Tweezing works too. Be sure to get the whole business end out of your skin.

And then there are chiggers.

Ivan Awfulitch

Chiggers strike terror in those who know all too intimately the insidious power of that invisible foe. Give me black flies, mosquitoes, ticks, no-see-ums, deer flies, horse flies, fleas, leeches, lice (well, maybe not lice) — anything, any pestiferous thing that feasts on human flesh in North America, but Lord, deliver me from chiggers!

Chiggers, known across the South as red bugs, are always (and accurately) spoken of in the plural. The grown-ups are beneficial mites that quietly munch on insects and insect eggs. But the kids make up for that parental goodness with a vengeance. When a suitable host wanders through chiggery foliage, the six-legged youngsters hop aboard for a brief visit. They scurry toward a comfortably warm, damp nook and bore into the host's skin to grab a quick lunch. Then they go back outside to play and metamorph and grow two more legs and do other chiggery things.

Later, the itch. A persistent itch which, when scratched, becomes a burning itch—one which insists on being scratched. An itch which wakes the sleeper, plagues the waking, intensifies in heat, and continues unabated for days. An itch displayed in random clusters of red bumps in armpits, under the belt line, beneath bra straps and brief bands, in crotch and navel, behind knees (even, heaven forfend, between toes, inside ears and, horror oh horror, on the scalp). Did I neglect to mention the cleft of bum? Yes — there, too.

For most folks, chiggers are a rare treat savored after a camping adventure or hike, a picnic or a fishing trip in the mitey woods. An unpleasantry to be borne and factored into future plans. (Commercial insect repellents work, as does dusting with flowers of sulfur, though they must be applied thoroughly and frequently to all potentially exposed surfaces.)

But consider this real-life horror story: What if your garden became a red-bug haven? What if the chiggers wouldn't go away—for years?

It happened to us, and the infestation has struck to the core of our beliefs. It would not be too strong to say that this ranks as one of the pivotal ethical dilemmas of my life.

Our garden contains a lovely collection of perennial flowers and savory herbs (if I do say so myself). They bloom from last frost to first, drawing visitors as blossoms do bees, and the weeding, the tending, the harvesting, the dead-heading are part of our daily ritual.

My partner and I have brought the full weight of our combined 50 years of organic-gardening experience to bear on this problem; we've searched libraries and the Internet and talked to extension-service experts.

We have clipped the grass short and roughed up the soil. We have liberally and frequently spread diatomaceous earth (a nontoxic, abrasive powder that scratches a bug's protective coating and dehydrates the critter). We have tried Safer brand insecticidal soap. Nada.

Last year, I phoned the Rodale Experimental Farm in Emmaus, Pa. —the home of Organic Gardening magazine—and talked to a researcher. Based on her advice, I paid $35 for a pint of Kleen Kill, a bioenzyme product, from a mail-order outfit in Tennessee. The chiggers laughed.

Swallowing hard, I bought some rotenone. For an organic gardener, using rotenone is really extreme. It is a broad-spectrum poison, though a "natural" one that dissipates quickly, thus minimizing damage to a garden ecosystem. Used as directed, it is generally accepted by the organizations that accredit organic farms. The chiggers didn't mind it either.

Today, however, I contemplate warfare. There are chemical poisons reputed to quell the savage mite. (I am Saddam, and the chiggers are my Kurds.) I must take care to avoid the place where the 10-year-old toad hangs out. I will do it on a warm, still evening—it must be dry before ground-feeding birds arrive at dawn. I will treat only the main pathways, avoiding overspray that could impact honey and bumble bees on nearby flowers. I will quit eating the mint, arugula and thyme that have spread from the garden beds into the walkway. I will feel wretched. It has come to this, or abandoning a 15-year-old perennial garden.

Damn, damn, damn.

(Reprinted from The Icarus Glitch: Another Duck Soup Reader, *Cecil Bothwell, Brave Ulysses Books, 2001)*

*(**Footnote, 2011:** This was written fourteen years ago, I don't recall what evil poison I used. It didn't work.)*

Flora

WNC is approximately unique in the world for the number and variety of species of plants growing within a small geographic region. The reasons are simple, though the impact is complex. Located in a temperate latitude and with elevations that run from 800' above sea level along the edge of the Piedmont to 6,684' atop Mt. Mitchell, the climatic range is breathtaking. We aren't far from either South Carolina's emblematic palmettos or Canadian evergreens and hardwoods in the high country. The Great Smoky Mountains National Park alone is home to over 100 species of trees.

Of particular interest to many hikers are almost 1500 species of wildflowers that bloom from early spring to late fall (May and June are typically the high point of the annual bloom). In addition there are more than 450 species of non-flowering plants. Because of the wide range in altitude and the huge variety in species, fall colors last a long time here, with the change generally beginning at higher elevations and working down the hillsides to the bottom lands. Whereas leaf season may last only ten days in New England, it can stretch past a month in WNC, from mid-September until the end of October.

Many of our trees are in trouble. The trees atop Mt. Mitchell and other high peaks have been dying in recent decades, due to severe air pollution and acid rain. It was first noticed among the red spruce trees, but now beeches and yellow birches are failing. Some areas look like a flameless forest fire has swept through, killing everything in its path. Flowering dogwoods, for whose May blooms this region is famous, are declining due to anthracnose, an imported fatal fungal disease. Eastern hemlocks, the most common evergreen in WNC are falling prey to the wooly adelgid, a tiny bug related to cottony cushion scale (familiar to many gardeners). The honey locust, a legume (related to green beans, and with a bean-like seed pod) has been increasingly prey to leaf miners in recent years, with most of the trees turning yellow and then brown in mid August.

All of these species seem to be following the lead of the American chestnut, which was wiped out by an imported blight in the early part of the 20th century. fortunately, a resistant strain of chestnut has been developed and the tree is being widely replanted. Some day, if global warming doesn't kill us all first, humans may once again see a climax forest of six foot diameter chestnut trees in these mountains.

Big trees are still to be found in many places. The most easily accessible grove of giants may be in the Joyce Kilmer Memorial

Forest (see Nantahala National Forest). Named for the author of the poem, "Trees," the easy, 1.9 mile loop trail leads you past 400-year-old trees, some 20 feet in circumference and over 120 feet tall. But there are stunningly large trees along many other trails throughout our region.

The U.S. Forest Service seems to prefer to pretend that old-growth doesn't happen here for the same reason that the USFWS downplays the mountain lions (see comments under Mammals, p. 98). It might affect their ability to sell timber below cost to the logging companies it subsidizes.

Fortunately a very dedicated environmentalist named Rob Messick spearheaded a documentation effort hereabouts. Leading teams of other volunteers, Messick hiked thousands of miles, over several years, to measure and map old growth stands. As a result, conservationists have solid data to back up their defense of the remaining ancient forest in our region. Go Rob!

Poison Ivy

Poison ivy grows luxuriantly in this climate. It forms great ropy tangles and climbs up gnarled trunks to flower in the treetops. When there is nothing to climb, the vine grows along and under the ground and supports leaves on erect stems. This form is known as poison oak. The plant produces a berry crop in the fall that is a significant food source for migrating birds. Unfortunately the sap of this plant produces an allergic reaction in most people.

The best way to avoid these deleterious effects is to learn to identify poison ivy. The plant has clusters of three, shiny, dark green

leaves (though between rains they may dull due to airborne dust). The stem tends to be covered with rootlets. These can sometimes be downright furry looking, and the stems also have surface sap that can trigger a reaction, even in mid-winter. If you accidentally touch it, see treatment ideas below.

The renowned natural foods expert, Euell Gibbons, described a method of immunizing oneself against the poison ivy allergy. **Use it at your own risk.** It worked for me (though immunity only lasts for one season)—and I am TERRIBLY allergic to the plant, sometimes even getting feverish as blisters spread all over my extremities. Utterly miserable.

Euell's method: On the first day you spy tiny poison ivy leaves sprouting from the bare winter stem, eat three leaves. Continue to eat three leaves every day for 21 days. (I picked them with rubber gloves, rolled them into balls and swallowed them whole, chased with a full glass of water.) At the end of these three weeks you will be eating three fully developed leaves. (Scary, eh?) I experienced a tiny amount of oral and rectal itching at about the mid-point of this process. I then pulled up hundreds of yards of poison ivy vines, in and around my garden, throughout a whole season, barehanded, and NEVER had an allergic reaction. I didn't do it the following season (most of the P.I. was gone from my yard), and experienced mild allergic reactions a couple of times. (I don't know if partial immunity continued, or if this was due to being generally careful not to touch the stuff.)

What to do if you get poison ivy

First, if you think you've touched it, rinse with plain water-no soap. Apparently water will flush away the oil whereas soap or detergent breaks it into smaller particles which are more likely to cause a rash.

A poison ivy rash can take up to a week to make its appearance and it's not picky about the season, you can pick it up from leafless vines in the winter.

Topical treatments include Oak-N-Ivy Brand Technu. Found at most drug stores, it's a wash to remove the oils and stop the itch. Ivy Dry is an old brand with many adherents. Jewelweed Lotion is another good remedy that can be obtained at health food stores to help with the itch and irritation. Calamine Lotion is proclaimed by many old timers as "the best thing for poison ivy", but it hasn't ever done much for me.

•**Why they call this Land of Sky: sunset over Grove Arcade**

The Weather

Let it rain, sweet Mary Jane

We get a lot of weather here in these mountains, yes indeedy. And whether you are a visitor or newcomer, you probably want to know what to expect. Don't we all?

The broad brush picture is this: we have a cool season and a warm season. The cool season is followed by a wet season and the warm season ends up pretty dry. Outside of the city it never gets terribly hot, and below 3000 feet it never stays terribly cold. Frost comes early and stays late in the valleys. Gardens on the east side of peaks never seem to get enough rain, while gardens on north slopes never get enough sun. Snow never sticks for very long (below 3000 feet) and heat waves are usually brief.

More than any other truism that might be offered concerning climatic conditions, this is gospel: **weather in any mountainous region is extremely local.** One valley can remain droughty while the next valley has a storm that turns it into a federally designated disaster area. Average annual rainfall hereabouts is 60 inches most of which falls when you are in fancy clothes and a long way from shelter without an umbrella.

In September of 2004 we played host to two southern visitors, Hurricanes Frances and Ivan, which pretty well whupped the river districts. Up to 20 inches of rain fell in 24 hours, leaving one big expensive mess. Mother Nature doesn't mess around when she's in a house-cleaning mood. For the next three years we experienced a devastating drought. In July 2009 as I write this we have just emerged from one of the wettest springs on record and have been warned that we are already tipping back into drought conditions. (This is what most computer models of global climate change predict: wider extremes, with heavier inundations interspersed with longer dry periods.)

Winter average lows range from 22°F in the northern mountains of to 28°F in Asheville. Average highs range from 44°F in the mountains to 48°F in town. Summer average lows run from 60°F in the mountains to 63°F in Asheville. During that season the average highs range from 82°F on the peaks to 85°F in town.

You might want to pack a sweater, a compact umbrella and an inflatable raft.

• *Train tracks in Biltmore disappeared below the raging Swannanoa River during the 2004 flood.*

Daddy's money
The trustafarians who built Asheville
by Cecil Bothwell

*"You should exercise a good degree of judgment in
determining who are proper objects of charity, and
who are not; there are impostors in the world, and
on that account many worthy persons have been refused
favors when they deserved them: But because there
are such, we are not to withhold, with a parsimonious
hand, from all who seek our assistance."*
-- James Patton, 1756-1845

There's a story making the rounds about street kids in Asheville: Sure, they look scruffy; sure, they've got totally matted dreads; sure, they've given up on straight society, capitalism, acquisitiveness, propriety and even bathing. But a lot of them actually have platinum-plus cards tucked in their backpacks. In other words, these faux freaks are really "trustafarians."

Seeking to track down the facts behind the tale, I talked to a dozen or so downtown store owners and clerks. But despite near universal agreement that there are trustafarians in Asheville, no one we spoke with could report having actually been handed a credit card by somebody who looked like home was a cardboard box or the Billy Graham Freeway overpass at North Lexington.

It could be a simple case of nearly irresistible urban legend, like the gators in the New York City sewers, or the noble soldier spat on by evil peaceniks. Wordspy.com offers this definition of trustafarian: "A jobless person who has access to money—especially a trust fund income—and who affects a laid back, bohemian lifestyle." The Web site traces the term's first use to The Washington Times back in 1992, and a Google search yields nearly 2,500 references to the word (many of which lend credence to the idea that it is merely a legend).

Then again, as a clerk at Malaprop's suggested, some of the more alternative-looking living-off-the-land folks who shop in Asheville might be mistaken for street people—thereby feeding the rumor, since they must have some level of means (whether inherited or earned) in order to own land. Or maybe the whole thing is merely the straight world's way of gaining reassurance that those free spirits who aren't punching a clock like the rest of us are really only faking it.

Of course, not everyone who inherits significant wealth is a scruffy sluggard; many of this city's greatest benefactors and most acclaimed citizens came into this world well provided for. And whether or not they qualify as bona fide trustafarians, a cruise through the local history books turns up a steady stream of such folks who left their stamp on Asheville.

The trailblazer

Forget about "best places" lists, retirees and tourism: Well-heeled immigrants to Asheville are not a recent phenomenon. In fact, the trend traces back to the man who was perhaps the first European to encounter these mountains. Born of nobility in Spain around 1500 and raised in comfort in Panama, Hernando de Soto had all the advantages that wealth and position can confer. He learned the ropes helping Francisco Pizarro destroy the Inca Empire. As Pizarro's ambassador to Atahualpa, de Soto befriended the captive Inca ruler and was utterly disillusioned when his boss accepted a huge ransom from Atahualpa—and then had him killed anyway.

De Soto left in a huff, taking about 18,000 ounces of gold (about $7.2 million in today's market) with him when he returned to Spain. But he was jealous of men like Pizarro and Hernando Cortés, who'd achieved fame as well as fortune. So, like so many future restless rich kids, de Soto made his way to Asheville. One of the wealthiest men in Spain—having lately married Isabella de Bobadilla, scion of one of the most renowned Castilian families—de Soto stopped in at the court of Charles V and offered to conquer Florida at his own expense. Charles obligingly named de Soto governor of Cuba (from where he sailed to Florida) and captain-general of any provinces he might secure by conquest.

In the course of de Soto's extensive adventures in the Southeast, historians believe he came through what's now Buncombe County. He was thus the first European ruler of this municipality— and arguably the first gold-card-bearing, longhaired, pale-skinned, rebellious young man to hang out in the Land of the Sky.

Reaching for the sky

Fast-forward several centuries to when James McConnell Smith, heir to his daddy's money (and 200-acre land grant), married Polly Patton and commanded his several slaves to build a bridge across the French Broad River -- and Asheville's first mansion. In his book *Historic Asheville* (Land of the Sky Books, 2001), local-history buff Bob Terrell writes that Smith built it for his son, John Patton Smith. John's daughter, Sarah Smith McDowell, and her husband bought the house after her parents died (women weren't allowed to inherit their parents' property in those days).

Today, the **Smith-McDowell House** (now a museum) is said to be Asheville's oldest surviving home and the oldest brick house in Buncombe County.

One of the next rich kids to make a really big splash in Asheville was Zebulon Baird Vance. The Vance clan couldn't hope to rival the de Sotos when it came to cold, hard cash. But their extensive land holdings set them well apart from the typical mountaineer of the time—particularly the Bairds' 9,000 acres, which included much of what is now the city of Asheville. Zeb doesn't precisely fit the mold of the young drifter who floats into town from parts unknown, since he only drifted down from a cabin in Reems Creek. But there's no doubt that family money and influence underwrote his career as a lawyer, congressman, Unionist, secessionist, slave owner, colonel, governor and finally a U.S. senator and first citizen of the region during and after the Civil War.

And more than a century later, we have Vance's soaring obelisk—a favorite gathering place for today's scruffy youth, whether true trustafarians or faux—to remind us that Zeb was here (which is more than de Soto has to show for his considerable efforts).

House-proud

The most famous trustafarian to land in WNC is unquestionably **George Washington Vanderbilt**. And despite his disadvantageous spot in the lineup, the eighth child of William H. Vanderbilt doesn't seem to have suffered financially.

During Asheville's first boom in the 1880s, George took to staying at the posh Battery Park Hotel. He fell in love with the mountains and began acquiring land to build his dream house. In his heyday, he owned 125,000 acres of woodland, give or take—a hefty chunk of what's now Pisgah National Forest, as well as Biltmore and Biltmore Forest. There he built what's still the largest privately owned home in the United States (the Biltmore House).

Vanderbilt's daddy was really loaded.

Grandpa Cornelius Vanderbilt was to railroading what Bill Gates is to computers; when Cornelius died in 1877, he was said to be the richest man on earth. He left $95 million of a cool hundred-mil fortune to his eldest son, William Henry. And by the time he died less than nine years later, William had managed to increase that tidy sum to about $200 million (those were 1885 dollars, mind you—and there was no income tax).

On William's death, his estate was divided among his four sons: Cornelius Vanderbilt II, William Kissam Vanderbilt, Frederick Vanderbilt and George Washington Vanderbilt (William Henry's daughters apparently had to fend for themselves by "marrying well"). In the usual manner of such bequests, George got a smaller share and had to make do with a mere $10 mil, according to the Archive Department at Biltmore Estate.

Like many of the kids on Lexington Avenue, George and wife Edith were frequent road-trippers. They were actually booked to sail on the Titanic but changed their minds at the last minute and switched to the Olympic. Most of their luggage, however (not to mention G's valet) went down with the famously doomed vessel. George lived two more years before succumbing during an emergency appendectomy.

But it wasn't all glitzy parties with the Vanderbilts, either: Edith's support for what became Biltmore Industries helped provide mountain families with much-needed income, and George's passion for forest management helped regenerate a portion of the region's blasted woodlands (now the core of Pisgah National Forest).

Forest for the trees

Nobody could match the Vanderbilts' wealth, but many tried —and few tried harder than the Packs. When **George Willis Pack** rolled into Asheville, he had deep pockets indeed. Daddy **George Pack** had founded the family timber empire when he sold his New York farm and moved to Michigan in 1848. He established a farm and purchased thousands of acres of timberland, opening his first mill in 1856.

His son, George Willis, took over the business in 1875 and continued to clear-cut a huge swath of old-growth forest in northern Michigan. Owning or co-owning at least eight mills, Pack amassed an enormous fortune. Just one of those operations—Pack, Woods & Company—cut 1.25 billion board feet of lumber before the trees ran out (as much as 78 million board feet per year).

George W. and his wife, Frances, moved to Asheville in 1888, buying thousands of acres in and around town; his extensive philanthropy soon made him the city's best-loved resident.

Their equally ambitious son, **Charles Lathrop Pack**, turned his father's substantial investments into even greater wealth, clear-cutting ever more extensive areas in the South (primarily Louisiana) and buying and selling land in Asheville. He even bragged to friends that he'd had the better of Vanderbilt in a deal involving a parcel that bisected the latter's vast holdings. According to biographer Alexandra Eyle in Charles Lathrop Pack: Timberman, Forest Conservationist, and Pioneer in Forest Education (Syracuse University Press, 1994), he "was one of the five wealthiest men in America prior to World War I."

Another son of wealth who drifted into WNC around the same time was **Gifford Pinchot**. Educated at private schools in Paris and New York City before attending Phillips Exeter Academy and Yale, he visited Biltmore Estate in 1891 and landed a job there as forest manager the following year.

Daddy James W. Pinchot was a successful New York City wallpaper merchant; his wife, Mary Eno, was the daughter of Amos Eno, one of New York City's wealthiest real-estate developers. Having seen well managed forests in Europe as well as the clear-cut wastelands that followed the sawyers' westward march across the North American continent, James turned his eldest son away from thoughts of the ministry and medicine, touting forestry as a more urgent pursuit.

But Gifford didn't stick around in Asheville for long. He divided his time between his business headquarters in New York City and assorted field locations where he worked as a consultant, in addition to his duties at Biltmore. By 1898 he was chief of the Forestry Division of the U.S. Department of Agriculture (which later became the U.S. Forest Service), and he twice served as governor of Pennsylvania (1923-27 and 1931-35). In the early 20th century, both Pinchot and Charles Pack (who ended up devoting most of his wealth to the cause of conservation) were at the forefront of American forest-preservation efforts.

Fine, you may say. But all that is ancient history: What about contemporary Asheville?

Julian Price moved here in 1990, saddlebags laden with his share of the Jefferson-Pilot insurance fortune (his grandfather founded two life insurance firms that later merged). Having spent the previous 20 years in Oregon and California as an organic farmer and photo technician while financially supporting environmental activism and recording cutting-edge interviews on diverse topics for public radio, the Greensboro native returned to North Carolina as a way of coming home—or nearly so.

While visiting Asheville, he was struck by the notion that this might be a place where he could do something different yet worthwhile. That general notion gradually evolved into a broad vision of philanthropy, which was grounded in his belief that downtowns should be livable and that regular people would benefit if he provided a financial boost to those working, often in small ways, to make downtown come alive.

Before his death from pancreatic cancer in 2001, Price was involved with too many projects and organizations to count. To support small, independent businesses and increase the amount of affordable housing downtown, Price created Public Interest Projects, a for-profit development company. At a time when few people actually lived downtown, Public Interest rehabilitated 18 buildings and created more than 75 housing units. Other for-profit beneficiaries of his money and enthusiasm included such downtown fixtures as Malaprop's Bookstore, the Laughing Seed Café, Jack of the Wood brew pub, NewEraCom, Salsa's Mexican Caribbean Restaurant, Zambra Wine and Tapas Bar, Green Line (a monthly newspaper) ... and even Mountain Xpress. In addition, more than 150 local and regional non-profits have received grants from the Dogwood Fund, which Price endowed through the Community Foundation of Western North Carolina. (This continuing charitable enterprise remains part of his legacy.) Among those groups are RiverLink, the Asheville Urban Trail, Citizens for Media Literacy, the Mountain Area Information Network, the Mountain Micro-enterprise Fund, the Preservation Society of Asheville and Buncombe County, Quality Forward, the Radio Reading Service; Pack Place Education, Arts and Science Center, the Self-Help Credit Union, City Watch magazine, the Pedestrian Action League and WCQS.

He didn't hang around the Vance Monument looking grubby, playing music and placing himself squarely in the face of passersby. Quite the opposite: Despite his remarkable impact on his adopted city, he preferred to shun the limelight. Few of the countless locals who directly or indirectly benefited from his largesse would have recognized Price—or even had a clue who he was—if they'd seen him on the street (as many undoubtedly did, since he lived downtown). And perhaps we would all do well to take a page from pioneering Asheville resident James Patton's book and "exercise a good degree of judgment" in assessing our neighbors, whether they appear to be ragtag or rich.

After all, this is Asheville.

This article first appeared in Asheville's weekly Mountain Xpress.
www.mountainx.com

• The stately Public Service building (center), located between Patton Avenue and Wall Street is just one of the properties given new life by Julian Price.

Asheville's monument to tolerance
Confederates, Jews join hands on Vance's birthday
by Steve Rasmussen

Zebulon B. Vance spoke movingly and influentially against what he called "the wickedness and the folly of intolerance." Rising skyward from the busy downtown crossroads of this Appalachian mountain town is an elegant spire of rough-hewn granite: the Vance Monument. Recently, Asheville's answer to the Washington Monument has been a focal point for controversy over nation-sized issues of war and freedom of speech, after police and city officials clamped down on the peace protests that, for months, had swirled around this memorial to North Carolina's own reluctant rebel.

The Vance Monument is more than just a shrine to a Civil War-era governor; more, even, than a forum for Asheville's remarkably diverse political views. Ever since the winter solstice day in 1897 when its cornerstone was laid (in a rare public Masonic ritual) to honor the Confederate Christian who stood up for the Jews, the monument has symbolized that most controversial of First Amendment rights: freedom of religion.

For more than a century – even in the dark days of the Ku Klux Klan's ascendancy, when hooded Jew-haters burned crosses and smashed **windo**ws in other Southern towns – the Asheville chapter of the United Daughters of the Confederacy has conducted a joint ceremony with the local chapter of B'nai B'rith each year at the foot of the Vance Monument.

What brings together such seemingly mismatched constituencies as a Southern-heritage organization and a Jewish-advocacy group on or about May 13 is the birthday of a Buncombe County native who probably did more than any other American statesman to prevent anti-Semitic prejudice from closing the nation's doors of immigration to a despised and persecuted people.

A voice for civil liberties
Zebulon Baird Vance, best known in today's history books as

North Carolina's governor during the Civil War, might seem an unlikely champion of religious tolerance. Like so many other native and adopted offspring of these mountains, however, the independent-minded Zeb Vance could not be confined to a narrow stereotype.

Born in 1830 in a log cabin in Reems Creek (now a state historic site), this son of a farmer and country merchant grew up to be a lawyer noted for his sharp and earthy wit. A U.S. congressman who was an eloquent supporter of the Union until the very outbreak of the Civil War, Vance chose loyalty to his home state once hostilities began. In Asheville, he organized the Confederate Rough and Ready Guards; as colonel of the 26th North Carolina Regiment, he gained such fame for his courage that he was elected governor of North Carolina in 1862 and again in 1864.

Vance's toughest fight as his state's wartime governor, however, was not against the depredations of Northern raiders but the draconian wartime dictates of his own government. When the Confederate Congress authorized President Jefferson Davis to suspend the writ of habeas corpus and indefinitely imprison Southern citizens suspected of "disloyalty" without trial, Vance declared that if North Carolinians were deprived of this constitutional right, he would "issue a proclamation recalling the North Carolina soldiers from Virginia, and call out the State's militia to protect the liberties of the citizens." The humanitarian governor also worked hard to improve the harsh conditions in which enemy prisoners of war were being held, and when it became clear to everyone except Southern leaders that the war could not be won, Vance pressed for peace with the North.

But it wasn't until the very end of the war, when a Jewish hat-maker rescued the captured Confederate governor from what could have been the most degrading moment of his life, that a profound respect for the despised Jews apparently first took root in Vance's heart. On his 35th birthday, Union cavalry surrounded the governor's home in Statesville and arrested him. The Union officer in charge was trying to force the portly and somewhat horsemanship-challenged Vance to ride or walk, in full public view, the 35 miles to the nearest rail line to Washington when Samuel Wittkowsky, a local Polish immigrant who admired Vance, intervened, persuading the officer to let him drive the governor in his carriage. The Southerner and the Jew became lifelong friends. After the war,

Vance won election to the U.S. Senate from North Carolina – but the Reconstruction-era Republicans controlling Congress refused to allow the ex-Confederate to take his seat. Forced to return to his law practice in Charlotte for several years until the political climate in Washington had moderated, Vance – most likely through

Wittkowsky – got to know and respect other members of that city's prospering community of recent escapees from Old World ghettos and pogroms. "The Scattered Nation" Around 1870, during his own exile from Washington, Vance composed "The Scattered Nation," a speech he would give hundreds of times to sold-out crowds in lyceums and lecture halls (the 19th-century forerunners of today's radio and TV talk shows) all across America in years to come, including his 20 years as a U.S. senator. Drawing on its author's oratorical gifts and wide reading in ancient and biblical history, the lecture makes a powerful case against what it calls "the wickedness and the folly of intolerance."

Vance opens with a striking comparison of the Jewish people to the Gulf Stream – a river of people moving through the sea of nations yet never mingling with it. He goes on to trace elements of such modern ideals as representative democracy and property rights to the ancient Hebrew tribal confederation, praising the lack of crime and the intelligence and strong family values he has personally seen among their modern descendants. Standing the anti-Semitic stereotype of the mercantile, ghettoized Jew on its head, Vance shows how, when persecution forced the Jews away from agriculture and land ownership, the "scattered nation" turned its hardships into virtues by establishing a system of universal commerce, based on mutual trust, such as could never have developed among the border-bound and language-divided "consolidated nations" of the gentiles.

Such arguments were eye-openers in an age when even educated Victorian Christians routinely stereotyped Jews as greedy Shylocks and thieving Fagins, refusing to allow even wealthy Jews into New York hotels – much less into such inner sanctums for political and economic decision-makers as the New York Athletic Club and Tuxedo Park (two places where Sen. Vance gave his speech).

Indeed, Vance is not above resorting to a Mark Twain-like gibe at Northerner stereotypes to get his point across: "Is there any man who hears me tonight who, if a Yankee and a Jew were to 'lock horns' in a regular encounter of commercial wits, would not give large odds on the Yankee? My own opinion is that the genuine 'guessing' Yankee, with a jackknife and a pine shingle, could in two hours time whittle the smartest Jew in New York out of his homestead in the Abrahamic covenant."

Vance reminds his listeners that the Jews were the source of their own faith: "All Christian churches are but off-shoots from or grafts upon the old Jewish stock. Strike out all of Judaism from the Christian church and there remains nothing but an unmeaning superstition." He also takes keen aim at religious bigotry, observing: "The popular habit is to regard an injury done to one by a man of a different creed as a double wrong; to me it seems that the wrong is greater coming from my own. To hold also, as some do, that the sins of all people are due to their creeds, would leave the sins of the sinners of my creed quite unaccounted for. With some, faith of a scoundrel is all important; it is not so for me." And just as the rising sun – which Vance says he's seen from "the summit of the very monarch of our great Southern Alleghenies" – disperses the night fogs that fill the mountain valleys, "so," Vance concludes, "may the real spirit of Christ yet be so triumphantly infused amongst those who profess to obey his teachings, that with one voice and one hand they will stay the persecutions and hush the sorrows of these their wondrous kinsmen."

Wreathed in galax

Two years after the widely admired senator's death in 1894, noted local benefactor George W. Pack offered to donate $2,000 to help pay for a monument to Vance in front of the Buncombe County Courthouse (then located on the east side of the current Pack Square). By 1898, the obelisk was complete. (A few years later, Pack proposed a more ambitious deal, offering to trade the county land for a new courthouse in exchange for its holdings on the public square, which would be "forever... held in trust for public use as a ... park" by Pack and his heirs.)

"To North Carolinians, he is the incomparable Vance of war and Senate fame and many jests; to the Jewish people he is the author of 'The Scattered Nation', the one American statesman of his day who pleaded their cause to the people of the United States," Vance biographer Selig Adler wrote in 1941. That advocacy, noted Adler, was all the more remarkable, given that "there were somewhat less than five hundred Jews in North Carolina at the time Vance wrote the speech, a fact that discounts all political motives." Jewish publishing houses repeatedly reprinted the famous speech.

And more recently, Maurice A. Weinstein's Zebulon B. Vance and "The Scattered Nation", (Wildacres Press, Charlotte, 1995) shone the spotlight on this remarkable story, helping keep Vance's memory alive among American Jews.

The same could not be said for many others, however. In the words of a 1930s-era story in the old Asheville Citizen on the "Colorful History Of Shaft On Pack Square": "As to the attitude of visitors to it, two contrasting stories may be told. A woman who has lived here all her life and is familiar with the story of the monument overheard two women on the street car: 'Who is the Monument to?' asked one. The other woman shrugged. 'Oh, some little local man, I suppose.' On the other hand many people will remember a wreath that used to hang on the monument: It was put there by a better informed visitor, a Jew who used to come to Asheville sometimes and who laid the wreath on Vance's Monument to honor the man who made the famous speech on the Jews."

That "better informed visitor" was none other than Jewish merchandising magnate/philanthropist Nathan Strauss of R.H. Macy Company fame, who came to Asheville shortly after World War I to lay a wreath on the monument because, he said, he did not want to die without discharging a debt of gratitude. It was Strauss, too, who arranged for the erection of the wrought-iron fence that still surrounds the obelisk, to fend off the loungers who even then frequented Pack Square. Strauss also left behind an endowment to pay for placing a wreath at the site each year.

Tradition holds that a member of B'nai B'rith was present when the United Daughters of the Confederacy laid the first wreath at the monument when it was dedicated in 1898. Forty years later, a photograph published in the Asheville Times shows representatives of the UDC, the American Legion and B'nai B'rith standing next to a sumptuous wreath (and behind the captured World War I German cannon that pointed down Patton Avenue until it was melted for scrap during World War II) as they unveiled a bronze plaque honoring Vance (which can still be seen on the monument's west face). Poignantly, the newspaper is dated May 14, 1938 – just a month and a day before the Nazis commenced "Operation June," a roundup of Jews who were unemployed or had committed petty administrative offenses (such as illegal parking or late payments); the victims were imprisoned in concentration camps until they agreed to leave Germany.

According to Sudie Wheeler, the former Vance Birthplace manager who now oversees the annual Vance birthday ceremony for the UDC, the wreath the Daughters of the Confederacy lay alongside the B'nai B'rith's is always made of galax leaves. (Galax, appropriately, is used by mountain herbalists to heal wounds.) "Some of the ladies did do a wreath and place it at the monument [at its 1898 dedication] with the galax leaves, and that's the reason we use the galax leaves today," said Wheeler. One unconfirmed story is that the leaves were traditionally gathered at a Black Mountain property formerly owned by Vance. In recent years, notes Wheeler, the ceremony has often been held at the Vance Birthplace or – as it will be this year – at Vance's grave in Riverside Cemetery, instead of at the downtown monument.

Most years, local members of B'nai B'rith still join the Daughters in the ceremony. Henry Meyers, the former state chairman of B'nai B'rith, speaks there nearly every year. To Jews, "what [Vance] represented was an understanding of where the Jewish place in the world was, and that having a Jewish population could enrich the general population," Meyers told Xpress. "He was a countervailing force against the evil of prejudice." And by saying to his fellow senators and congressman what no Jew was allowed into the exclusive clubs and fraternities where they gathered to say, notes Meyers, Vance kept America's doors open to Jewish immigrants such as the Russian parents of Jonas Salk, who developed the polio vaccine.

"Vance was making sure that the Jews were understood for what they were – that all they needed was a place where they could flourish. And some of those people who flourished were amazing," Meyers observes. "No Vance, no Salk."

This article first appeared in Asheville's weekly Mountain Xpress. www.mountainx.com

Another view

"Like his parents, Vance owned a small number of slaves. And while he's often remembered as a progressive leader, at least for his times, McKinney makes it clear that Vance was 'an avowed racist who used the racism of other whites for personal advantage and political purposes.'

"In March of 1860, for example, Vance rose before the House of Representatives to argue that blacks were genetically inferior and to rail against the idea of race-mixing. "Even the mind of a fanatic recoils in disgust and loathing from the prospect of intermingling the quick and jealous blood of the European with the putrid stream of African barbarism," he said."

From Jon Elliston's review of Gordon B. McKinney's biography, Zeb Vance: North Carolina's Civil War Governor and Gilded Age Political Leader *(University of North Carolina Press, 2004),* Mountain Xpress, *Jan. 19, 2005.*
www.mountainx.com

New Age Nazi
The rise and fall of Asheville's flaky fascist
by Jon Elliston

The news quickly crossed the Atlantic, hitting the United States like an ill wind. Adolf Hitler had vaulted into power, becoming Germany's chancellor. Most Americans familiar with Hitler's National Socialist German Workers' Party reacted with apprehension, but one Asheville man was "inspired," as he would later put it. William Dudley Pelley—writer, publisher, guru, self-proclaimed metaphysician and avid anti-Semite—was about to hitch his fate to the Nazis' rising star.

Pelley was working late in his Charlotte Street office that day when his secretary brought in the evening paper. In his autobiography, The Door to Revelation, Pelley recalled how he'd seized on the front-page headline about Hitler. "I looked at the lines. I read them again. I sought to comprehend them. Something clicked in my brain!" Pelley had been watching Hitler for years, admiring the man who'd railed against the "Jewish menace" and muscled his way into power with a cadre of brown-shirted thugs. As a few of Pelley's compatriots milled about the office, he looked up from the newspaper and made an impassioned announcement that stopped them in their tracks. "Tomorrow," Pelley declared, "we have the Silver Shirts!"

And that's how, on Jan. 31, 1933, Asheville became home to what would prove to be one of the largest pro-Hitler organizations in the United States: the Silver Legion of America (or Silver Shirts for short). Their brief and bitter story is an unusual one for Asheville, and their mercurial leader's news-making career here is all but absent from most local histories.

That lack of attention, plus other recent disclosures about the strong but historically hidden and overlooked ties between some prominent Americans and the Nazis, makes Pelley's story seem ripe for review. No less a personage than President Bush's grandfather, the late Prescott Bush, has come under new scrutiny for his part in bankrolling Hitler's rise to power. And a new book—Max Wallace's The American Axis: Henry Ford, Charles Lindbergh, and the Rise of the Third Reich—shows how even those two American icons served as pro-German propagandists.

It's a history that can be hard to come to terms with, Wallace told me in a recent phone interview. "We look at Hitler's Germany as a sort of lunatic operation, as the kind of thing that just couldn't happen here," he said. "People are embarrassed to think that Americans could have embraced this lunacy."

It was, of course, only a brief and partial embrace. Today, Asheville displays no memorials to Pelley, no monuments or street names to mark his legacy. But amid the current wave of historical investigations of American ties to the Nazis, the special-collections division of UNCA's Ramsey Library recently made available a set of files documenting much of Pelley's work in Asheville. In addition, Pack Memorial Library has long housed rare Pelley materials, including most of his books and well-preserved copies of Silver Shirt newspapers. From those faded pages and yellowed news clips emerges the long-forgotten but still-intriguing story of Asheville's New Age Nazi.

Pelley's purpose

Although he achieved notoriety here, Pelley was not an Asheville native. He was born in 1890 in Massachusetts, the son of an itinerant Methodist preacher turned toilet-paper manufacturer. A restless but contemplative boy, Pelley showed a talent as a wordsmith from an early age. At 19, he launched his first magazine, The Philosopher, and he would remain a prolific publisher for the rest of his life.

In his 20s, Pelley freelanced for popular magazines, including Collier's, Good Housekeeping and The Saturday Evening Post. Soon his writing started taking him places. Pelley covered the aftermath of the Russian Revolution in Siberia as well as historic events in the Far East. Back in the United States, he won prizes for his short stories, penned several novels, and struck gold in Hollywood, where he cranked out a series of screenplays that were made into major motion pictures. Despite those accomplishments, though, Pelley wasn't satisfied.

Something was missing, he felt—some sense of deeper purpose. He found it one May night in 1928 when, while sojourning at a California mountain bungalow, he drifted into what he later described as an "ecstatic interlude." For "seven minutes in eternity," Pelley said, he left his earthly body and entered a mystical realm where he bathed in an ornate pool "among jolly, worthwhile people," including a divine oracle who continued to speak to him from then on.

"Call it the Hereafter, call it Heaven, call it Purgatory, call it the Astral Plane, call it the Fourth Dimension, call it What You Will," Pelley wrote in an account of the episode. "Whatever it is—and where —that human entities go after being released from their physical limitations, I had gone there that night." Feeling reborn into a fundamentalist form of Christianity, he decided it was his mission to "give the whole race an inspiration by which it may quicken its spiritual pace."

In search of further insight, Pelley abandoned Hollywood for a brief stint in New York City, where he networked with clairvoyants and mystics of all sorts. Frequenting Greenwich Village salons and séances, he quickly developed what was to prove a lifelong interest in a grab bag of esoterica, from channeling to pyramidism, from studies of the afterlife to extrasensory perception, weaving it all into his unique brand of Christianity.

In 1930, Pelley relocated to Asheville, where, with assistance from wealthy donors inspired by his spiritual revelations, he founded the short-lived Galahad College. Housed in the Asheville Women's Club building at the corner of Charlotte Street and Sunset Parkway (today the site of the Zion Christian Assembly church), Galahad offered a course of study based on Pelley's own developing philosophy. Key courses included "Christian Economics" and "Social Metaphysics." Meanwhile, Pelley launched a new magazine, Liberation, which featured his latest insights obtained from the "hyper-dimensional instruction" he said he received via "mental radio." Along with flowery paeans to Jesus Christ, the newspaper featured articles with titles like "Why You Are Opposed by Invisible Persons," "Take Your Daily Cues From the Great Pyramid" and "You Can Remember Before You Were Born!"

Galahad College folded after a couple of years, but Pelley continued to churn out his mystical manifestos. Meanwhile, he began searching in earnest for a way to parlay his supernatural interests into some tangible power here on earth. It wasn't long before another mystic with political aspirations, one Adolf Hitler, paved the way for Pelley's most ambitious project yet.

Silver Shirts

In 1933, grabbing onto Hitler's coattails, Pelley shifted his focus from spiritualism to fascism. "Silver symbolizes the purity of our fight," he proclaimed, "and the purity of our race." The Silver Shirts, he vowed, would wage "the ultimate contest for existence between Aryan mankind and Jewry."

Pelley's writings, one critic declared in a 1934 New Republic article, were now "a mad hodge-podge of mystic twaddle and reactionary, chauvinistic demagogy." Jews, Pelley maintained, were the source of all the world's supposed evils, from Communism to "Hebrew Jazz." In Washington, he wrote, "Jewish vampires" were pulling the levers of power through their pawn, President Franklin Delano Roosevelt.

In kinder times, this bigoted world-view might have been wholly disregarded. But in pockets of Depression-era America, hard times had prompted a rise in scapegoating—and the Jews were a ready target. For some, Pelley's peculiar brand of hate-mongering— still interwoven with his idiosyncratic strain of mystical Christianity —struck a sympathetic chord.

Good timing wasn't the only way Pelley seemed tailor-made for the role of American führer. Like the German leader, Pelley was a short (5 feet 7 inches) and oddly dapper man. Sporting spectacles and an angular goatee, he clad himself in the uniform he designed for the Silver Shirts: a silver or gray shirt with a scarlet "L" above the heart (to signify the "Legion"), a blue necktie, short-cut blue corduroy pants, and black leggings covering the tops of black boots. At rallies, Pelley donned a gray cap modeled after the ones worn by Hitler's storm troopers, and he was judged a rousing (if pompous and bombastic) orator.

As he threw himself into organizing his own "SS," Pelley was delighted to find ready recruits across the country. "It was an awe-inspiring thing," he wrote in his autobiography. "I had known that the nation was disgruntled with the encroaching caste of Jewry. I had never appreciated that it hungered for leadership like this." Chapters of the Silver Shirts sprang up in 22 states, with the largest clusters organizing in the Midwest and on the West Coast. At its peak in the mid-1930s, Pelley boasted that the group's membership reached 25,000; historians, however, have put the number closer to 15,000.

Establishing a quasi-military command structure, Pelley designated himself "chief" and appointed state commanders across the nation. The rank and file were grouped into 10-member "safety councils" that were instructed to meet regularly and learn to act as a unit. While a few Silver Shirt chapters conducted serious paramilitary training, most busied themselves with listening to speeches, holding the occasional public rally or march, and distributing Pelley's many publications.

In the pages of Liberation and Pelley's Silvershirt Weekly, the author trumpeted his plan for addressing "the Jewish problem"—a plan that bore no small resemblance to Hitler's. The Silver Shirts, Pelley pledged, would spearhead a new "Christian Commonwealth" in the United States, which would register all Jews in a national census, then systematically reduce their role in business, government and cultural affairs, ultimately confining all Jews within one city in each state.

"We are sanctioning no programs of mob violence in dealing with this people," Pelley wrote to his followers in 1934, "but by the same token we are not ignoramuses in regard to Judah's plans and purposes and we will not stand for nonsense." In fact, for all their hostile rhetoric, the Silver Shirts rarely became involved in violence, and when they did, Pelley's followers didn't generally fare well. Militant trade unionists and Jewish gangsters sometimes sent their own strongmen to break up Silver Shirt rallies. According to a report by the American Jewish Historical Society, for example, Minneapolis "gambling czar" David Berman and his associates forcibly shut down three Silver Shirt gatherings, "cracking heads" and effectively running the group out of town.

And though the organization brought a core of devoted activists to Pelley's crusade, even at its peak, the Silver Shirts remained a fringe group mostly ridiculed by both the national and local press. A 1934 Asheville Times editorial, for example, openly mocked Pelley: "Asheville enjoys the rather dubious distinction of being the headquarters of the Silver Shirts. This honor was not achieved, but thrust upon the city. ... We have seen the Silver Shirt movement for what it is. In laughing at it, we laugh at others who find it a menace to the Republic."

Pelley, however, could claim genuine success in at least one pursuit: His anti-Semitic ruminations spread nationwide. Pelley's print shop, housed in the old Biltmore-Oteen Bank building, cranked out such items as the 10-cent pamphlet <I>What 50 Famous Men have Said About Jews<I> and a 25-cent reprint of The Protocols of the Learned Elders of Zion, a turn-of- the-century anti-Semitic forgery—already discredited by reputable scholars by the 1930s—that purported to reveal a "Jewish plot against Christian civilization."

But the strongest salvo in Pelley's war of words was another forgery, the so-called "Franklin Prophecy," which he appears to have authored. The Feb. 3, 1934 issue of Liberation featured an unattributed article, provocatively titled, "Did Benjamin Franklin Say This About the Hebrews?" The article reproduced a lengthy excerpt from what it claimed was the diary of South Carolina's Charles Pinckney, one of the framers of the U.S. Constitution. Purportedly written during the Constitutional Convention in Philadelphia, the "diary" entry recorded Franklin saying that while the new country must guard against religious tyranny, a more severe threat was at hand: "This greater menace, gentlemen, is the Jew!"

The entry quoted further from Franklin's supposed screed, which urged barring Jewish immigration to the new United States: "In whatever country Jews have settled in any great numbers they have lowered its moral tone. ... If you do not exclude Jews for all time, your children's children will curse you in your graves!" A dramatic declaration, to be sure—but a fictitious one. There's no evidence that Franklin ever made those remarks, much less that Pinckney ever wrote them down, according to numerous subsequent historical investigations of the "Franklin Prophecy." Still, the forgery —appropriated by Germany's propaganda apparatus—echoed around the world.

Shell games and sedition

For all Pelley's energy, vision and skill as a propagandist, however, he proved to be an abysmal businessman. With each new political or 122 Bothwell&Ball spiritual whim, it seemed, Pelley founded another enterprise, never pausing to solidify any of them. In the course of a mere 10 years, he incorporated Galahad College, the Galahad Press, the Fellowship Press, the Foundation for Christian Economics, the League for the Liberation, Pelley Publishers and the Silver Shirts, and founded five publications: Liberation, Pelley's Silvershirt Weekly, The New Liberator, The Galilean and Roll-Call.

Congressional investigators later concluded that the Silver Shirts had raised some $174,000 in the 1930s through donations and publication sales. But Pelley badly jumbled the finances among his various endeavors, conducting a contorted corporate shell game that promptly mired him in legal troubles. In January 1935, Pelley was found guilty of selling worthless stock. Convicted of fraud in Buncombe County court, he was fined and given a suspended prison sentence.

Meanwhile, the federal government was also casting a wary eye on the Silver Shirts. In 1934, the House of Representatives' newly created Special Committee on Un-American Activities sent an investigator to Asheville to seize a sizable portion of Pelley's financial records. (Later, in 1940, the committee would call Pelley to Washington to grill him about his pro-Hitler organizing and publishing.)

Undaunted, Pelley rallied the Silver Shirts behind a madcap bid for the White House. In 1936, he ran as the presidential candidate for the hastily assembled Christian Party, whose platform resembled the Silver Shirts' hate-filled mission statements. Pelley campaigned in 16 states but made it onto the ballot in only one: Washington state, where he garnered a mere 1,598 votes (300 less than the Communist Party candidate received).

As the United States drifted closer to war with Nazi Germany, Pelley and other American fascists pushed to keep the country neutral and openly backed the Axis powers. Meanwhile, early in 1941, Pelley decided to relocate. His legal problems in Asheville had multiplied, and worse, he'd attracted no significant local following, outside of his small circle of advisers and office staff. He was just getting his new headquarters off the ground in Noblesville, Ind.—strategically positioned amid some hotbeds of Silver Shirt activity—when the United States declared war against Germany and Japan.

Although Pelley was clearly too marginal a figure to pose any real threat to national security, President Roosevelt himself now deemed the Silver Shirt leader a menace to society. In January 1942, Roosevelt wrote FBI Director J. Edgar Hoover, mentioning Pelley's publication The Galilean and commenting, "Some of the stuff appearing therein comes pretty close to being seditious." The president added, "Now that we are in a war, it looks like a good chance to clean up a number of these vile publications." In a March cabinet meeting, Roosevelt went further still, ordering Attorney General Francis Biddle—a civil libertarian who'd been reluctant to crack down on dissenting publications—to move against Pelley.

The FBI raided Pelley's offices in April 1942 and arrested him. In August, a jury of farmers and tradesmen in Indianapolis federal court found him guilty on multiple charges of sedition. The trial featured at least one laughable moment: While Pelley was on the stand, his attorney accidentally addressed the Silver Shirt leader as "Mr. Hitler." Further into the mystic Sentenced to 15 years in prison, Pelley spent the rest of the war behind bars. Paroled in 1950, he returned to writing and publishing but mostly steered clear of politics. Pelley spent his remaining years in Indiana, delving further and further into mystical explorations. He founded a small, cultish group called Soulcraft and spent thousands of hours writing messages "channeled" from various deities and expounding on the divine providence of UFOs and extraterrestrials.

Despite Pelley's ignominious descent into the dustbin of history, it would be wrong to say his influence died with him. The fraudulent "Franklin Prophecy" he fostered has found new life on the Internet via neo- Nazi Web pages and online discussion lists. In fact, Pelley was a kind of founding father of modern hate groups, as several former Silver Shirts went on to become instrumental in forging the post-World War II white-power movement. In the early 1970s, for example, Henry "Mike" Beach, a former Silver Shirt state leader, co-founded the Posse Comitatus, a violently racist anti-government group. And former Silver Shirt Richard Butler, now 85, has spent the last 30 years leading the Aryan Nations, until recently the country's most prominent neo-Nazi organization.

In Asheville, however, the sole vestiges of Pelley's work are stored away in libraries. And that should come as no surprise, observes UNCA history professor Milton Ready, who helped assemble the university's Pelley collection. "He did not have a base of support here," says Ready. "This was just a mail drop for him." Asheville was simply too tolerant, he says, and its Jewish community too involved in business and civic affairs, for Pelley-ism to take root locally. By the time Pelley died in 1965 at age 75, he had faded into near obscurity. There was, however, one final, fitting tribute to the man who'd stoked the fires of fascism in America. Shortly after Pelley's death, as his body lay in state in a funeral parlor near Indianapolis, someone planted a wooden cross in the ground outside and set it aflame.

This article first appeared in Asheville's weekly Mountain Xpress.
www.mountainx.com

Gentlemen, start your memories
Locals claim their place in racing history
by Brian Sarzynski

Thomas Wolfe once wrote a book about his hometown – making fun of a lot of people and telling some tall tales in a language resembling English, thereby pleasing a bunch of Yankee literary types while pissing off the locals to the point that they ran him out of town. But time heals all wounds, or so they say: Wolfe's Asheville home is now a museum. We even named an auditorium after the guy.

Banjo Matthews, on the other hand, lived in west Asheville for many years, never went to college, lived hard and drove fast – and chances are he never read *Look Homeward, Angel*. Matthews, though, had an uncanny ability to fix cars. Actually, he could do more than just fix them – he could take mass-produced "stock" cars and turn them into thundering beasts of speed. He's been called the Henry Ford of race cars and a maestro mechanic.

On the NASCAR circuit, Banjo accomplished the following: From 1974 to 1985, cars he built won 262 of 362 Winston Cup races. In 1978, his cars won all 30 races held by NASCAR that year. Oh, and he could drive, too.

In fact, after winning 13 consecutive races at one Asheville track back in the 1950s, the track promoter asked him to "back off." It seems attendance was dropping because the outcome of the race was a given if Matthews was running. Being a man of pride and honor, Matthews refused to throw the race – but he did agree to be handicapped. So the promoter started him in the back of the pack – with his car facing backward, no less. When the green flag dropped, Matthews spun his car around, passed the pack and, yes, won the race. And that, my friends, is the stuff of legends.

Local racing left to rust

Today, however, your average Asheville resident couldn't tell you a thing about old Banjo (who didn't play his namesake instrument, by the way). There are no museums named in his honor. No auditoriums. Not even a filling station. Zilch.

Racing, it seems, has been all but erased from Asheville's cultural persona – except among the surviving older members of the local racing community. Flip open any glossy magazine promoting tourism and you'll see ads touting Asheville's temperate climate, its arts scene, its architecture – or else a picture of some buff guy kayaking. But it's pretty doubtful you'll see a grease monkey bent over the hood of a '47 Ford up on blocks – though the sight was a common one around here, back when a generation of post-World War II Ashevilleans found recreation and empowerment through horsepower.

That cultural amnesia, however, is reversing: Regional racing stories and memories are now being captured for posterity. And in the process, a posse of pioneering locals is finally getting recognized for being in the vanguard of what's now become a national phenomenon. This past summer (2003), the west Asheville library hosted a discussion series on the history of stock-car racing in Buncombe County.

The first meeting found a handful of former drivers and fans swapping stories about racing – but the series quickly evolved into a popular oral history project recorded on 10 CDs. The stories, hopefully now preserved forever, are a free-flowing account of the early days of stock-car racing.

• **Driver Dickie Plemmons poses beside his car after a race (mechanic and photographer unidentified; photo courtesy of Mrs. Dickie Plemmons).**

And the tales literally roared in – from Fairview's Hollywood Road Track to the Asheville-Weaverville Speedway (a near-perfect oval that Gene Sluder carved out of his farmland with a keen eye and a tractor). Old-timers relived the insanity of racing souped-up cars around McCormick Field's baseball diamond, and the rise and painful demise of the New Asheville Speedway (later renamed the Asheville Motor Speedway).

But sweet or bitter, the memories couldn't have surfaced at a better time. Today, NASCAR has surpassed baseball and basketball in popularity – that is, if TV ratings and memorabilia sales are any indication. And as stock-car racing continues to disperse from its Southern roots and spread across the country, the mighty NFL could be the next to fall.

NASCAR's fan base is now estimated at around 75 million. Between its premier Winston Cup Series and its (for want of a better term) minor leagues – the Busch Series, the Craftsman Truck Series and the regional circuits – NASCAR now offers 1,800 sanctioned races a year across 38 states. Even stock cars' premier sponsorship has recently traded hands: from the R.J. Reynolds Winston cigarette company to the Nextel Corporation (the naming rights cost Nextel a cool $700 million). On top of that, NASCAR is in the middle of a six-year, $2.4-billion broadcast contract with both the Fox and NBC networks.

Tobacco and Tar Heels may have made NASCAR, but in the 21st century, racing has gone high-tech – and it's eagerly distancing itself from any hint of redneck. There's barely a square inch on a modern stock car that isn't covered with a sponsor's logo – in some circles, the motto is: "Race on Sunday, sell on Monday." But whether Madison Avenue likes it or not, stock-car racing owes an enormous debt of gratitude to a generation of men who made their home in the mountains of Western North Carolina and the foothills of the piedmont.

Meeting history head-on

The story of stock-car racing is steeped in oft-told tales of moonshine- running, shade-tree mechanics and men who brawled as hard as they drove. How much of it is truth and how much is lore is hard to discern. But when that history is told in the time-honored tradition of Appalachian storytellers, trivial matters such as veracity take a back seat to the necessity of spinning a good yarn.

One rich tale recounts a spectacular crash at a local speedway. Banjo Matthews and Ralph Earnhardt (Dale's dad) had been trading paint all night, neither driver wanting to back off in front of the screaming fans. Coming out of the final turn, Matthews gave Earnhardt one last kiss on the bumper and sent him careening off the track – and straight into the first-base dugout.

Yep, the dugout. And if you think this writer is mixing his metaphors, or simply confusing baseball terminology with racing slang, well, you obviously don't know much Asheville sports lore.

Ralph Earnhardt – the patriarch of one of NASCAR's most fabled families – crashed into the dugout, as did many other drivers who dared to run their stock cars on the quarter-mile track that circled the bases at Asheville's storied McCormick Field.

As one of baseball's oldest ballparks, McCormick is, to most locals, synonymous with the Asheville Tourists. Having hosted the Babe, Jackie Robinson, Willie Stargell and a scrawny batboy named Cal Ripken, McCormick Field is part of the fabric of our national pastime. But during a brief three-year period in the 1950s, baseball abandoned Asheville, only to be replaced at McCormick by the upstart sport of auto racing. The temporary conversion of the diamond into an oval proved a smash hit – resulting in a whole lot of smashed cars – much to the squealing delight of the local racing fans who packed the stands.

Asheville Citizen-Times writer Bob Terrell recently described the appeal at one of the library's racing roundtables: "With 25 cars starting on a quarter-mile track inside a baseball park ... well, something just had to give." But while Terrell's comment hints at the motorized mayhem at McCormick during those years, one could easily interpret the remark as a prescient summation of the erosion of baseball's popularity in the region – and the rise of its four-wheeled, uniquely indigenous replacement. Something did have to give way, and the loser ultimately ended up being the Grand Old Game, which gave way to auto racing as the South's supreme sport. However, baseball returned to McCormick – much to the relief of the park's many neighbors, who vociferously griped about the racket from the downtown racetrack.

"Back then, we didn't have face shields" Haw Creek resident Ed Cox raced at McCormick and recently shared some of his stories with me. Asked what it was like to race around the bases on four wheels, he grinned broadly. "Ever heard of a demolition derby?" he queried. "I remember one time I went end over end three times and hit the right-field wall." Cox, a mechanic by trade, raced at all the local tracks – and even some places that didn't quite fit that description. "We used to race in some farmer's cow field," he recalls. "Back then, we didn't have face shields – you never knew if what was hittin' your face was dirt or a cow pile."

As for the current state of the sport he helped create, Cox readily points out, "There's no resemblance. "Back then, we built our own cars, and you could build a pretty good one for under $2,000," he explains. "Today, the cars cost millions before they even see a track – these guys have 15, 20 guys on a crew, a support team with a garage back home, and all sorts of money from sponsors. "Nobody ever approached me and asked to put their name on my car," comments Cox. "It's become too commercialized, like Christmas and Easter. Everybody's forgotten what they're all about. They've taken the real meaning out of it. Racing used to be just a bunch of country boys having a good time. "They're racing for real money now," he muses. "Back then, you could win a race, and get a check for winning, and you still lost money. A hundred dollars was a big check, but you'd have more than that [invested] in your car."

Minding the Intimidator

Max Wilson is a retired U.S. marshal with enough stories about chasing crooks to fill a Hollywood screenplay. Locally, though, Wilson is known as one of the founders of the New Asheville Motor Speedway on Amboy Road. When he was still in his early 20s, he and some partners pooled their funds to buy a privately owned airstrip down by the river. The way Wilson describes it, Asheville's last racetrack was born out of the dreams of young men with few resources and an abundant willingness to take risks. Avoiding a catastrophe was the last thing on their minds.

"All we had was a paved runway for the planes. We didn't have any money to build the track, so I said, 'Doggone it, let's have us some drag racing on the runway and sell tickets to raise money to build the track.' "The other guys agreed, and we started the first weekend with drag racing. We did [it] every Sunday. But I was worried we'd get hundreds of people showin' up and gettin' real close to the runway – and some of those cars were going 80 miles per hour. Someone was gonna get hurt.

"So we took out insurance every weekend," Wilson reveals. "The only insurance company that would touch us was Lloyd's of London. So we'd send them a certified check for $160, postmarked the Friday before each race. It was a standing agreement. Four times we sent that money in. But we were real hard up for money – and we hadn't had any accidents, no complaints, everything real smooth. So on the fifth weekend, we didn't send the money in.

"That Sunday," he recalls, "I was standing on the back of a truck at the end of the runway announcing the races on a loudspeaker. Suddenly, I Finding Asheville 129 heard this roar and looked up and saw this big ol' plane flying across the field. I said to myself, 'Surely he's not thinkin' about landing here with 1,400 people lining the runway. I don't reckon he'd be that stupid.' He disappeared over the trees and I started the next race.

"Then, the next thing I know, the plane is back and he's got his landing gear down – almost hit me in the head. So I told everyone to get back and I jumped off the truck. Just then, his wheel clipped something – a speaker wire, I think – tore the wheel clean off and sent it flying over the concession stand. It didn't hit anyone, thank God.

"But now the plane's landing on one wheel in the middle of all these people – [it] hits the runway and goes this way and that, carving a trench into the runway the whole time with the side of the plane missing a wheel. It comes to a stop at the end of the runway – didn't hit a single person and all nine people on the plane were fine. Turns out he'd run out of fuel and had an old map that listed the place as an airport.

"Next damn weekend, we sent that insurance money in."

Wilson also talked at length about his gig as a babysitter at the speedway. "I told Ralph Earnhardt that I'd give him $80 show money to come up from Kannapolis to race here in Asheville. You know, if we got rained out, Ralph would give the money back. And he needed it, but that was the kind of guy he was. Anyways, Ralph didn't have no crew – he was everything: mechanic, driver, tire changer – the only person he'd travel with was his boy.

"Dale was only 6 or 7, but was he fascinated by cars! Ralph was scared he'd get killed roaming around the track while he was racing. So I'd watch him with my wife in the office while the race was on. Dale was real bad about minding me. I'd turn around and he'd be gone – off wandering around those cars.

"You couldn't tell him nothin'!"

This article first appeared in Asheville's weekly Mountain Xpress. www.mountainx.com

In fall of 2010, a NASCAR memorial was unveiled at Carrier Park, on the site of the former race track. From the south, take the Amboy Road exit from I-240 E. From the River Arts District, take Riverside to Amboy, turn right.

Asheville's Afro-History
The missing stories
by Cecil Bothwell

Like many other cities in the American South, Asheville has a checkered history in regard to race relations, with moments and movements of confluence and community separated by long periods of distance and discord. Thanks to the dedicated public efforts of people working through churches, schools, the YWCA and our home-grown Building Bridges program, as well as the quiet work of photojournalists and oral historians, we have recently seen some progress in tearing down barriers and honoring our hidden past.

In the years following the European invasion of Cherokee lands there were four significant periods of voluntary black settlement in the French Broad River basin. In the late 1600s some blacks accompanied Indian traders as workers and over the next century a few stayed on. Then in the 1830s, following completion of the Buncombe Turnpike, trade increased and with it came a diverse group of drovers. Again in the 1880s, jobs opened up with the coming of the railroad, drawing now-free blacks in larger numbers. And then again at the turn of the century, a burgeoning tourist trade offered service jobs to non-whites.

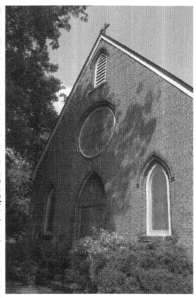

A larger number of blacks arrived as slaves. The pre-Civil War slave population of Asheville included an estimated 40 percent of perhaps 1,000 city dwellers, and slaves built some of the oldest extant structures here, including the Smith-McDowell House. Following the Emancipation Proclamation, some of that number stayed on though many migrated west and south. Three black churches were established in the late 1860s: St. Matthias Episcopal (photo), First Nazareth and Hopkins Chapel African Methodist Episcopal Zion

Church. The churches became the linchpins of the growing enclave.

The coming of the railroad in the 1880s brought tourists and trade with its attendant service jobs—the only jobs available to most non-whites, but the railroad also left a legacy of further distrust and alienation. Black convicts were hired out to the rail company and were worked like slaves, with many dying while performing the dangerous work of blasting a rail bed over the pass from Old Fort to Black Mountain. Given that racial bias played a major role in arrest and conviction (then as now, though hopefully to a lesser degree), to some it appeared that *de facto* slavery had replaced *de jure*. Still, there were jobs to be had and at the turn of the century an increasingly successful and tight-knit black community began to emerge. Two black newspapers were founded as well, the *Mountain Gleaner* and *The Enterprise*.

Private and parochial schools were created in tandem with the churches and in 1887 the school board, including black business owner Isaac Dickson, opened the city's first public schools—one for whites and one for blacks. (Today, one of Asheville's elementary schools bears Dickson's name.) In 1892, George Vanderbilt provided $32,000 in construction funds and enlisted Asheville's most famous architect, Richard Sharp Smith, to design the Young Men's Institute as a community center for his black employees. The magnificent pebbledash structure of the YMI remains the cultural center of Asheville's black community. (And, having worked on a remodeling project in the building in 2009, this writer/carpenter can attest to the superior construction of the building. Vanderbilt spared no expense.)

Continued pressure from the black community and increased resources available in the early boom years led to creation in 1923 of WNC's largest secondary school for blacks, the Stephens-Lee High School, whose graduates would soon number among leaders and professionals in the region, with many becoming members of a growing black middle class and an important part of the 1960s civil rights movement here.

In the 1920s the Eagle/Market Street district, adjacent to the YMI, was at the center of a flourishing commercial section of town. New professional offices were built for black businessmen, medical doctors and dentists and other trades. During this decade there was an annual, week-long "Colored Fair," more or less modeled on what we know today as a state fair, which drew visitors from all over the region for farm- and home industry-displays, music, dancing and "aeroplane stunts."

Night clubs were founded which carried on for the next three decades and hosted nationally famous musicians including Louis Armstrong, James Brown, Duke Ellington, Ruth Brown, and Fats Waller. "The Block" as it became known, was jumping! In the 30s an annual "Negro Music Festival," co-sponsored by many white and black organizations, raised funds for projects for "Negro children," and drew audiences numbering up to 800 which included equal numbers of whites and blacks.

As Tom Kerr noted in *The Underground Asheville Guide Book*, "Prior to the mid-1970's, downtown was home to one of the hottest African American music scenes in the nation and attracted both regional and national acts. Sam Cooke, James Brown, Aretha Franklin, Otis Redding, Chubby Checker, Chuck Berry, Bo Diddley, B.B. King, Sam & Dave, Willie Dixon, and other famous performers visited Asheville to play venues like the Orange Peel." The Orange Peel was later converted into a roller-rink, then abandoned, and reconverted to a music club in 2001.

To place that in context it's worth remembering that American popular music was probably the most thoroughly integrated profession in mid-century. While black patrons were not permitted in whites-only clubs and ballrooms, the jazz and dance bands that played in those venues were often black or integrated, and whites could and did patronize black venues. Oddly, perhaps, as society desegregated in the 1960s and 70s, the music world fractured: white musicians moved into multi-track studio recording while blacks continued to produce dance music, with the former moving into folk-, pop-, country-, and cosmic-rock, while R&B segued into soul, disco, hip-hop and rap. (Though there were and are cross-over artists.) Most music was listened to from recordings and dance halls like the Orange Peel died, finally reemerging as concert venues in the 21st century.

Because the city was still strongly segregated in mid-century the black community provided all of it's own services and businesses, leading to establishment of many successful enterprises and growing wealth. However, as Nan Chase notes in her superb volume, *Asheville: A History* (McFarland, 2007), that wealth was very relative. Using 1941 data from the Buncombe County Tax Assessor's office she points out that the 75 percent white population owned 20 times the dollar value of property compared to the one quarter non-white, and that figure doesn't include local railroad or utility holdings —also white owned.

In 1956, two years after Brown v. Board of Education had helped launch the modern civil-rights movement, Eleanor Roosevelt agreed to speak in Western North Carolina—but only if she could address a racially mixed audience. The venue for the former First Lady's talk was the Asheville YWCA—which was emerging as a leader in the local push for integration. However, like most other YW's in the country, the organization still maintained separate facilities for whites and blacks. It wasn't until 1968 that the Asheville branch became the first officially integrated YWCA in the South and another two years before the black and white organizations were actually consolidated under one roof. Even then there was considerable opposition and the *Asheville Citizen* reported, "Making one YWCA out of two when the basic ingredients are black and white is proving about as easy in Asheville as mixing oil and water."

Segregation extended to most shared public spaces. Starting in the 1920s and continuing until about 1970, water fountains and rest rooms, as well as bus and train waiting areas were strictly separate, as was theater seating. While writing a 2007 biography of evangelist Billy Graham, this writer interviewed numerous old-timers in the black community who still harbor deep resentments for Graham's exclusion of non-whites from his Asheville crusade events in the 1950s. "He was willing to take our money when we donated," said one, "but he wouldn't let us come to his meetings."

At other Graham events during that period, blacks were admitted but relegated to a balcony (as they were in most movie theaters.) The late Dr. John P. Holt, an Asheville native and second generation physician as well as school board member, told me, "He made us sit up in the balcony, but that's the way it was back then. It's what we expected."

The Fine Arts Theater, on Biltmore Ave., has preserved its "colored" entrance, a small, separate ticket window and entry door

leading to the balcony, as a reminder of the reality of segregation in this city. And, as local poltical activist Jesse Junior reminded viewers in a recent video about that era, those balcony patrons had no access to popcorn or beverages.

Thinking back to the 1960s, Holt also remembered Graham's father-in-law: "Nelson Bell lived one block from our house on College Street," Holt recalled. "I can remember walking right by where he lived almost daily. He was a tall, good-looking man and the leader of The John Birch Society in town. At the time, the Birch Society was very prominent because the anti-civil rights attitude was beginning to develop. and John Birch was the most anti-civil rights organization in Asheville."

(During the 1960s, The John Birch Society opposed the Civil

Rights Movement generally, alleging communist influence, and the 1964 Civil Rights Act specifically, asserting that it was in violation of the Tenth Amendment —the reservation of otherwise unspecified powers to the states or to the people. There were close ties to the Ku Klux Klan and across the South it was often accepted wisdom that the JBS was the public face of the more secretive KKK, though members heatedly denied the connection when confronted.)

At the time, Holt served on the School Board and was helping to negotiate the desegregation of Asheville's school system. When that occurred in 1967 it was a first in the South and a feather in Asheville's cap, one step forward in a region that had seen far too many steps back. However, for many in Asheville's black community, desegregation was a very mixed blessing. The history and pride associated with Stephens-Lee High School were subsumed into Asheville High School and students formerly educated by black instructors were suddenly thrust into mostly white classrooms with white teachers who were, no matter how excellent, not racially relevant role models, and at worst were closet racists bridling at the forced integration of their schools. The black dropout rate ratcheted upward and has yet to come back down.

Partly because blacks were forced into self-reliance because of separatism, racism and poverty; and partly due to the cohesive centrality of the black churches, the post WWII African American community was tight-knit. But the bonds of family and commerce that were so very real to those citizens weren't particularly visible to the ruling white elite. Where the community saw itself as prospering within its allotted niche, white leaders saw poor quality buildings, shacks with chickens and pokeweed in the yard, and lots of room for improvement. Soon enough that led to a new fracturing along a still tectonic racial divide.

Urban renewal was the road to perdition for many U.S. communities during the 1960s, paved as ever with good intentions, and pavement it was. First Asheville's Southside community was depopulated and razed to make way for ticky-tacky housing projects, then, in 1979, the East End community was bulldozed beyond recognition. Valley Street, once the principal north-south corridor through Asheville's black residential district, was cleared and re-made into a major transit corridor as an extension of Charlotte Street and renamed South Charlotte. As an additional kick in the teeth, it came to be known that the namesake "Charlotte" was not that other WNC city, but the daughter of Thomas A. Patton and Patton had owned slaves.

College Street was widened across the north side where the recently completed I-240 had blasted through Beaucatcher Mountain in parallel with College.

Government office buildings were strewn along the west side of Charlotte during ensuing decades, including the widely mocked "Taj Ma Garage." An office complex sprang up adjacent to the College Street tunnel entrance along with other commercial buildings. The East End was no more. Meanwhile hospitals and associated doctors' office complexes filled in formerly black neighborhoods on either side of Biltmore Avenue and down to McDowell, completing obliteration of much of Asheville's historic African American community. A few of the original churches endure, marking old intersections of that missing community.

The Eagle/Market Street district remains as a shadow of what once flourished to the east and south, and today serves as a focal point for remembrance, both via the YMI Cultural Center exhibits and events and through the annual Goombay festival which draws thousands of visitors to celebrate black culture each August. A planned renaissance of the Eagle/Market district has been touted by the city for several years but has been slow coming to fruition. Three great restaurants have set up camp in recent years (see the restaurant listings on page 62).

One response to the ongoing divisions between black and white communities in Asheville was creation of Building Bridges in 1993. The nine week program is designed to both educate and to facilitate discussion at a very personal level with an emphasis on cultural diversity and community building. Sessions begin with presentations by speakers or relevant films, then break up into small groups, created to maximize racial and age diversity. The process deepens as friendship and trust develop and I can attest that after taking the course twice I have had my eyes opened, have engaged in soul searching, and have greatly diversified my circle of friends.

Building Bridges has deeply affected people and institutions throughout Western North Carolina. To date, more than 1200 participants from throughout WNC have attended the program which is offered in a different venue each time: churches, schools, health facilities and UNCA have all sponsored the series over the past sixteen years.

(The success of the program has spawned copy-cat programs in other cities across the country. For more information visit: www.buildingbridges-asheville.com)

Finally, to end this brief history on a postive note, there has unquestionably been great progress in race relations in Asheville in recent decades. As of this writing, Mayor Terry Bellamy, the first African-American to hold Asheville's highest office, is running for re-election unopposed, and a few other blacks have been elected to Council through the years. Barriers have been knocked down in city government and school system hiring (though the teaching staff remains overwhelmingly white.) Other African Americans hold the chair of the county Republican Party and a vice-chair of the Democratic Party. Our annual Martin Luther King Day Breakfast has had the highest attendance of any MLK Day event in the U.S. in many years, with speakers drawn from across the nation. and the local chapter of the NAACP is active and growing. The black owned *Urban News and Observer* has emerged as a strong voice in the now multi-racial downtown community.

Sunday mornings remain the most segregated hours of the week here, as in most of America, but cooperation between churches is on an upswing. The diverse Interdenominational Ministerial Alliance is active as is Christians for a United Community, which works to build common ground. We can surely do better, but we have more than begun.

Cake out in the rain
Tanker leaks liquid uranium
by Cecil Bothwell

One of the hundreds of truckloads of radioactive material that pass through Asheville each year was seen leaking on Friday, June 25. A passing motorist spotted liquid dripping from the tanker as it sped along rain dampened Interstate 26 on its way from the Nuclear Fuel Services manufacturing plant in Erwin, Tenn., to the Savannah River Site near Aiken, S.C. The motorist phoned the N.C. Highway Patrol, which intercepted the trucker and sidetracked him at the weigh station between Fletcher and Hendersonville.

Paperwork provided by the driver indicated that his cargo was uranyl nitrate and Henderson County Emergency Management was called in to evaluate the situation. Emergency Management Coordinator Rocky Hyder told *Xpress* that the leak was small. "Something less than a pint leaked while the truck was at the weigh station." Uranyl nitrate is a liquid form of yellowcake uranium; dissolved in acid, it's used to manufacture reactor fuel and weapons-grade fissionable material. After processing at Savannah River, the same uranium may travel back through Asheville headed for the Oak Ridge Reservation Y-12 bomb factory. A tanker carrying 1,000 gallons of 1 percent uranyl nitrate would carry about 800 pounds of uranium ... tankers containing 3,000 gallons of 4 percent uranyl nitrate routinely traverse Asheville's interstate highways.

Nuclear Fuel Services referred questions about the incident to the Creative Energy Group, an advertising and public-relations firm in Johnson City, Tenn. Tony Treadway, the agency's president, told *Xpress* that the concentration of uranium in the liquid was "less than 1 percent." Asked how often such shipments pass through Asheville, Treadway responded, "It's very irregular for a shipment of that concentration to come through." Xpress: "How often do NFS trucks carrying radioactive material come through Asheville, North Carolina?" Treadway: "We can't share that information. Since Sept. 11, we don't share a lot of that information, for obvious reasons." Asked the same question, Hyder replied, "I'm not sure of the exact number, but I would expect we have shipments coming through here every day."

A tanker carrying 1,000 gallons of 1 percent uranyl nitrate would carry about 800 pounds of uranium, according to calculations based on information in Federal Register environmental documents available on the EPA Web site. According to the same documents, tankers containing 3,000 gallons of 4 percent uranyl nitrate routinely traverse Asheville's interstate highways.

Lou Zeller, executive director of the Blue Ridge Environmental Defense League, an environmental group, told Xpress, "This week's spill is but one in a long series of accidents involving radioactive materials. State and federal agencies routinely issue statements saying, 'no danger,' regardless of the facts. But radioactivity is an invisible and odorless poison, and few people have geiger counters. So, it's easy to cover up the damage. The bottom line is: There is no safe level of radioactive exposure."

This article first appeared in Asheville's weekly Mountain Xpress. www.mountainx.com

Pigeons after exposure to ionizing radiation.

Alphabetical Index

10,000 Villages..............................22
16 Patton...............................32p.,55
2 S. Pack Square..........................87
2 South Lexington Ave................74
A Boy and His Dog................22, 57
A Far Away Place.............19, 20, 32
A Touch of Glass..........................29
Adorn...23
Aesthetic Gallery...................22, 57
African-American history..........142
airport..16
Akzona Building...........................26
Albers, Anni 56
Albers, Josef...........................56, 91
Altamont Theatre..........................87
American Folk Art & Framing....56
antiques...25
Appalachian Craft Center............57
architecture...................................36
Ariel Gallery.....................27, 33, 56
Armstrong, Louis 143
art...55
Art Deco................................36, 39p.
art galleries......22pp., 27, 29, 32, 55
art supplies...................................58
art walks.................................50, 53
Asheville Art Museum.27, 33, 42p., 55
Asheville Pizza and Brewing62, 74, 76
Asheville Civic Center.....18, 30, 80
Asheville Community Theatre.....87
Asheville Discount Pharmacy......22
Asheville Fish Company..............25
Asheville Gallery of Art.........22, 57
Asheville Mural Project...............31
Asheville Wine Market................27
Asheville Yacht Club...................22
Asheville: A History....................144
Atelier...23

Barley's Taproom14, 33, 45, 63, 74, 76, 80
Basilica St. Lawrence.....18, 36, 41, 58, 94
Battery Park 17
beads..20, 23
Beads & Beyond....................20, 32
Beans & Berries.....................25, 34
Beanstreets....................................24
Beanwerks Coffee & Tea.......28, 34
Beaux Arts....................................36
Beaver Lake..................................43
beer..22
Beer Joints....................................74
beer, local..................22, 32, 63, 65
Bele Chere.....................................51
Bell, Nelson 145
Bella's...19
Bellagio Everyday.......................33
Bellamy, Terry 147
Bender Glass 58
Berry, Chuck 144
Bier Garden...............................73p.
biking..45
Biltmore Avenue. 14, 16, 26, 33, 38, 45, 63, 67, 80
Bio-Wheels...................................45
birds..99
Bistro 1896...................................26
black history...............................142
Black Mountain College Museum & Art Center...................25, 56, 91
Black Bird Frame & Art..............58
Blackley, Laura 79
Blaze n Skyy 19
Blue Meanies................................48
Blue Ridge Environmental Defense League......................................150
Blue Ridge Parkway.........16, 93,94
Blue Spiral 1 Gallery.............27, 56

BoBo Gallery.............24, 57, 74, 80
Bonnie's Little Corner.................18
book sellers................................91
Book Works...............................29
books..............................18, 23, 32
Botanical Gardens......................43
Bouchon 24, 63
breakfast all day.........................73
Brew Pubs.................................74
Brewgrass Festival......................77
Broadway. 16, 23pp., 30, 33, 51, 67, 80p., 85p., 90
Brodsky, Chuck 79
Brown v. Board of Education....144
Brown, James 143
Brown, Ruth 143
Bruisin' Ales.....................30, 74, 77
Building Bridges................142, 147
Buncombe Turnpike...................142
Burgermeister.............................28
Burke, Hillarie 59
bus depot...................................16
bus tours...................................47
Cafe Ello.............................32, 34
Cage, John 56
calendar (free annual events).......48
Candlestation.............................61
Captain's Bookshelf..............18, 92
Carmels' Restaurant and Bar.......18
Carolina Cigar Company.............18
Carolina Lane................24, 56p., 59
Cats and Dawgs...................18, 45
Celtic Way..............................20, 32
ceramics (do it yourself)..............20
Chamber of Commerce..................8
Chase, Nan K...........................144
Chatsworth Art & Antiques.........57
Checker, Chubby 144
Cherokee..................................142
Chevron Trading Post & Bead Company..................................23
Chai Pani..................................19

children's merchandise................18
chocolate...............................19, 25
Chocolate Fetish...........................74
Chorizo......................................18
Christians for a United Community 148
cigars..18
City Bakery...................27, 33p., 63
City building...............................36
City parking lots 13
City/County plaza.................36, 52
Civil Rights Act.........................146
Clark, Sherri Lynn 79
Climbax 42
Clingman Cafe............................60
clothing.........................20, 24p., 33
Coffee Shops..............................34
coins...18
Colburn Gem and Mineral Museum 27, 33
Cold Mountain...........................90
College Street Pub......................22
Compleat Naturalist...................101
Concerts on the Quad.................50
Cooke, Sam 144
Cookies by Design......................74
copy shop..................................18
Corner House.......................22, 39
Cornerstone Minerals..................23
Cosmic Vision............................23
Costume Shoppe.........................23
Cotton Mill studio......................61
Cottonwood Café........................27
Craft Brewers Brewgrass Festival 77
crafts, local...............18, 27, 32, 57
Craggie Brewing.........................76
Creeley, Robert 56
Crucible Glass Works............24, 56
Cucina 24 Restaurant and Bar.....20
Cunningham, Merce 56
Curve Studio..............................61

Daddy's Money.................20, 37, 39

de Kooning, Elaine 56

de Soto, Hernando 118

desegregation............................146

dessert...74

Diana Wortham Theater..27, 33, 81, 87

Dickson, Isaac 143

Diddley, Bo 144

Digable Pizza...............................28

Dirty Jack's............................74, 75

Dixon, Willie 144

Dobra Tea 24

Doloros Jose Mina Mexican Restaurant....................................29

Double Decker Coffee Bus..........27

Downtown After Five..................49

Downtown Books and News.23, 31, 57, 92

Drhumor Building........................39

Dripolator..........................25, 34, 81

drum circle.....................22, 48, 66

du Plessix Gray, Francine 56

Eagle Street......................27, 38, 52

Eagle/Market Street...................143

Early Girl Eatery........20, 46, 64, 73

earrings...................................18, 32

EarthGuild....................................58

East End....................................146

Ellington, Douglas 36, 39

Ellington, Duke 143

Emancipation Proclamation.......142

Emerald Lounge...........................81

Enter the Earth.............................18

Everyday Gourmet.......................33

family outings..............................42

family restaurants........................45

Feathers & Needlepoint...............19

Fiesta Latina 52

Fine Arts Theater..........27, 56, 145

Finkelstein's Loan.......................25

Fired Up!.....................................20

Firestorm Cafe & Books.22, 28, 34, 82, 92

First Nazareth............................142

Fitzgerald, Zelda..........................88

Flat Rock Playhouse....................87

Flatiron Building.................18p., 39

flora..112

Flying Frog............................27, 64

Forever Tattoo..............................24

Franklin, Aretha 144

Frazier, Charles 90

Freaks and Geeks Tattoo Sideshow 28

Free entertainment.......................48

Free Planet Radio.........................79

French Broad Chocolate Lounge 25, 32, 34, 74

French Broad Brewing 74

French Broad Food Co-op...........27

French Broad River..............95, 142

Frog Bar and Deli...................64, 73

Front Gallery....................27, 33, 55

Fuller, Buckminster 56, 91

Funky Mutt..................................23

Gaea..23

gallery crawl................................53

gargoyles.....................................37

Giant Crystal Under the City 10, 11, 12, 22, 83

Goombay.............................52, 147

Gothic...37

Graham, Billy 145

Great Smoky Mountains National Park..............................9, 16, 94

Greek Festival.............................52

Green Light Cafe.........................24

Green Man Brewing Company....75

Green River.................................96

Green Sage Coffeehouse........24,33

Grey Eagle Tavern & Music Hall 60, 82

Grove Arcade......17, 21, 34, 40, 58,

115

Grove Arcade Copy Shop............18

Guastavino, Rafael 41

Guergarian, River 79

guided tours.....................43, 45, 96

Guthrie, Arlo 82

Haen Gallery.........................27, 56

Hairspray..............................82, 86

Hanger, Howard 21

Harvest Records.........................29

Haynes, Warren 79

Headwaters Outfitters..................44

Health Adventure.............27, 33, 42

Hearns Cycling...........................45

Hedgepeth, Byron 79

Heiwa Shokudo..........24, 31, 46, 64

Heller, Stephen 79

Highland Brewing.......................77

Highwater Clays.........................60

Hip Replacements.......................24

Holcombe, Malcolm 79

Holt, David................................79

Holt, Dr. John P. 145

Honeypot...................................24

Hope-Gill, Laura 59

Hopes, David 59

Hopkins Chapel African Methodist

Episcopal Zion Church..............142

ice cream.......................12,18p., 74

Image 420..................................29

In Your Ear Music Emporium......28

Indo Apparel and Gifts...........27, 42

Indulgences...............................19

Instant Karma.............................23

Interdenominational Ministerial

Alliance....................................148

Interstates 26, 40, 240.................16

Izzy's Coffee Den............24, 29, 34

Jack of the Wood.20, 22, 63, 65, 74, 76, 82, 122

Jackson Building.........................37

Japanese fare..............................46

Jerusalem Garden.......22, 65, 66, 73

jewelry..............................18, 20, 58

Jewels That Dance.......................58

John Birch Society.....................145

Jonas, Billy 79

Jubilee! Community....................21

Junior, Jesse 145

Kamm's Kustard....................18, 74

Kane, Christine 79

Kanpai Sushi 26,65

Karmasonics....................27, 33, 83

Kathmandu.................................22

Kerr, Tom 144

Kilwin's Chocolate Fudge & Ice Cream...............................19, 74

King, B.B. 144

Kismet Café & Coffee House 34

Kline, Franz 56

Kottke, Leo 82

Kress Building............................38

Kress Emporium.........................32

Ku Klux Klan...........................146

Kubos Japanese Sushi................26

L.O.F.T................................25, 56

La Catrachita..............................29

La Empanada..............................29

Lake Julian.................................44

Lake Lure...................................96

Lamkin, Josh 79

LaMotte, David 59, 79

Larkin, Patty 82

Laughing Seed Cafe...46, 63, 65, 73

Laura Blackley Band,.................79

Laurey's Restaurant & Catering..27, 33

LaZoom Comedy Tours 47

Lexington Ave. Brewery..24, 74, 77

Lexington Avenue Arts & Fun Festival.....................................52

Lexington Street....................20, 92

lgbt...25

Licklog Players..........................87

Limones.................................27, 65
Lipinsky Auditorium....................50
Liquid Dragon Tattoo...................24
Littlest Birds.................................28
Lobster Trap............................66, 73
Look Homeward, Angel.............88p.
Loretta's.......................................22
Lucky Dog Studios......................29
Lucky Otter...........................29, 66
Mac Kah, John 61
Mad Tea Party.............................79
Malaprop's Books and Café..32, 46, 58, 83, 92
Mamacita's.................27, 33, 46, 66
maps...16
Martin Luther King Day Breakfast 148
Mast General Store.................27, 33
Mayfel's............................22, 66, 73
Mediterranean Restaurant............22
Mela.........................24, 46, 67, 91
Mercado Mexicano.......................29
Mid-Day Musicals.......................51
Miles Building.......................19, 39
Miles, Fred 39, 41
minerals................................18, 23
Minx......................................24, 28
Mission at the Grove...................18
Mo' Daddy's...............................83
Mobilia..58
Modesto..18
Moelietha's Shoes.......................28
monarch butterflies......................31
Montford Park Players...........50, 87
Moran, Laura 59
Morgan, Stephanie 79
Mountain Gleaner.......................143
Mountain Lights...........................23
Mountain Made...........................18
Mountain Renaissance Adventure Faire...49
Mountain Sports Festival.......49, 93

Moving Sidewalk Tours 47
murals...30
Namasté Yoga..............................25
Nantahala Gorge..........................96
NASCAR....................................136
NASCAR memorial...................141
Natural Home..............................23
Natural Selections.......................19
natural world...............................99
Navé, Jim 59
Navitat Canopy Tours 44
NC Stage Company 87
Nest Organics, next in line,.........23
New French Bar...........26p., 67, 73
Nine Mile.....................................67
Noland, Kenneth 56
Noodle Shop................................26
O. Henry......................................90
O.Henry's....................................86
Octopus Garden...........................24
Odyssey Center for the Ceramic Arts,...60
Old Europe..................................24
Old North State............................25
Olive or Twist..............................25
Olson, Charles 56
Ophelias......................................27
Orange Peel..................25, 83, 144
Orbit DVD...................................28
Orengo, Ozzie 79
organic goods........................23, 27
OrganicFest.................................52
Origami Ink and..........................58
outdoor ctivities 30
Outfitters.....................................96
Over Easy Breakfast Cafe......67, 73
Overstrøm Studio Fine Art 20
Pack Memorial Library....27, 43, 51
Pack Place 14, 27, 33, 42, 51, 81, 87
Pack Square....16, 22, 26, 38, 42, 81
Pack, George Willis.............37,120
Pack. Charles Lathrop 120

Pack's Tavern.............................37
Paris French Bakery.....................34
parking......................................13
parking FREE 14
passenger rail service...................16
Patton, Thomas A. 146
Paul Taylor Custom Sandals &
Belts...20
Penland School............................56
Penn, Arthur 56
pet stuff.....................................19
pharmacy...................................22
Phil Mechanic Building...............61
Pinchot, Gifford 120
Pineapple Jack's..........................29
Pisgah Brewing...........................77
plants.......................................112
poison ivy.................................113
Posana Cafe 26
Price, Julian 121
Pritchard Park. .16, 21p., 26, 32, 38,
48, 66, 92, 94
Pro Bikes.............................28, 45
Pub Prowl.....................11, 63, 65
Public Interest Projects..........20, 39
Public Library.............................43
Public Service 39
Public Service Building...............20
Purl's Yarn Emporium.................20
rafting.......................................44
Railside Studios...........................61
Ramsey, Tyler 79
Rauschenberg, Robert 56
Redding, Otis 144
Redmond, Glenis 59, 90
restaurants (recommended)..........62
Richard Sharp Smith..............38, 41
Richards, M.C. 56
River Arts District.......................60
River District Studio Strolls.........50
River outfitters............................96
Riverlink....................................61

Riverside Cemetery.....89p., 94, 127
Roberto Coin...............................18
Robinson, Dana and Susan 79
Rockburne, Dorothea 56
Rocket Club................................83
Roger McGuire Green.................37
Romanesque Revival...................39
Roosevelt, Eleanor 144
Rosetta's Kitchen...................24, 67
Rosser, Chris 79
S&W Cafeteria............................39
salons..23
Salsa Mexican-Caribbean......26, 68
Sam & Dave..............................144
SART...87
Satchel's Bar.........................22, 39
Sazerac......................................68
Scandals 86
Schrader, Connie 59
Scully's......................................24
secret passage.............................21
Second Gear................................29
Segway Tours..............................47
Self Guided Tours.......................35
Self Help....................................20
Shahn, Ben 56
Shakespeare in the Park...............50
Shindig on the Green...................50
Short Street Cakes 29. 74
Silver Dollar Diner......................60
Simple Gift.................................30
Sisters McMullen...................33, 34
Skateboard Park...........................45
slaves.......................................142
Smith-McDowell House....119, 142
Smith, Richard Sharp 38, 41, 143
smoke shops.....................24, 32, 78
Smoky's After Dark.....................25
Sons of Ralph..............................79
Southern Appalachian Repertory
Theatre......................................87
Southern Waterways....................44

Southside.....................................146
Spanish Baroque Revival.............41
Spellbound Children's Books 20, 92
Spiritex....................................22, 23
St. Matthias Episcopal...............142
Steak & Wine.......................22, 39
Steep Canyon Rangers................79
Stella Blue...................................84
Stella's...84
Stephanie's Id.............................79
Stephens-Lee High School.........143
Stevenson's Rare Coins & Jewelry
....18
Street Fair..............................18, 32
Studio Five Imports.....................33
Sugar Momma's Cookies.............74
Sunday brunch 73
Sunnypoint Café&Bakery 29, 68, 73
Suwana's Thai Orchid............24, 69
Swannanoa River.........................95
Table..69
Tallgary's Pub 81
Tastee Diner................................29
tattoo...24
Terra Diva..............................24, 30
Thai Basil....................................18
The Block...................................144
The Dripolator............25, 34, 74, 81
The Hop 28, 74
The Laughing Seed Restaurant....20
The Market Place...................20, 66
The New French Bar 26
The Wedge studios......................61
Thirsty Monk......................22, 75p.
Thirteen Moons...........................90
Thomas Wolfe. 35, 37, 88pp.,90, 94, 136
Thomas Wolfe's father................37
Three Dog Bakery.......................19
tiendas latinas.............................29
Tingle's Cafe...............................69
Tolliver's Crossing Irish Pub........28

Tops for Shoes.............................23
toys...23
transportation.............................16
Tressa's Downtown Blues & Jazz
.....................................25, 85, 86
trolley tours.................................47
True Blue Art..............................58
True Confections.............18, 34, 74
Tudor...38
Tupelo Honey Cafe 22, 69, 73
Twombly, Cy 56
Ultimate Ice Cream 74
UNCA....................................43, 50
Underground Asheville Guide
Book..144
Universal Joint 28
Urban News and Observer........148
urban renewal.............................146
Urban Trail.................21, 35, 39, 43
Va-Va-Voom...............................19
Van Dyke Jewelry & Crafts...27, 55
Vance Monument....16, 26, 35, 37p.
Vance, Zebulon Baird....38, 119,123
Vanderbilt, George Washington. .18, 37, 55, 143, 119
vegetarian restaurants...................24
Vigne,...25
Vincenzo's Bistro and Ristorante 27, 69
Virtue..24
Wadopian, Eliot 79
Wall Street...14, 19pp., 32, 39p., 42, 46, 64pp., 122
Waller, Fats 143
Warehouse Studios.......................61
Warren Wilson College...............91
Wasabi...25
weather......................................115
Wedge Brewery.....................61, 75
Weinhaus.....................................22
West Asheville.....16, 28, 34, 45, 85
West End Bakery.............28, 34, 70

Westfest..49
West Village Market 28
Westville Pub.............28, 70, 73, 85
Westwood Galleries.....................29
Wicke & Greene Estate Jewelry. .20
Wilcox, David 59, 79
wildlife....................................43, 99
Willem, Willem............................56
WNC Nature Center..............43, 99
Wolf, Allan 59, 90
Wolfe, Thomas 35, 37, 88pp., 94, 136

Wonderland.................................32
Woolworth Walk....................30, 58
World Coffee....................19, 32, 34
Write On.......................................23
yarn..20
YMI Cultural Center......27, 37, 143
Young Men's Institute..........37, 143
YWCA—...........................142, 144
Zambra Wine and Tapas Bar..30, 70

East Fork, Pigeon River, oil on canvas, by the author
(Can you find the hidden trout?)

Also by the author

A thoughtful and probing consideration of the ways in which our beliefs determine behavior, diet, resource use and habit.

The second edition of the only critical political biography of the world's most famous preacher. In this internationally acclaimed volume the author examines Graham's relationship with presidents from Truman to Obama.

This is not the story of a man of peace.

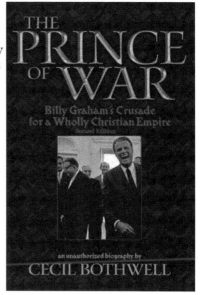

About the author

Cecil Bothwell was elected to the Asheville City Council in 2009. He's a writer and biographer based in Asheville and has received national and regional awards from the Association of Alternative Newsweeklies and the Society of Professional Journalists for investigative reporting, criticism and humorous commentary. He is former editor of *Asheville City Paper*, former managing editor of Asheville's *Mountain Xpress,* founding editor of the Warren Wilson College environmental journal *Heartstone*, served for several years as a member of the national editorial board of the Association of Alternative Newsweeklies and is a board member of two educational nonprofit organizations working in Latin America. His weekly radio and print journal, *Duck Soup: Essays on the Submerging Culture*, remained in syndication for ten years. He lectures widely on subjects ranging from environmental issues to ethics, the misguided war on drugs, and the necessity of separation of church and state.

He blogs at: http://bothwellsblog.wordpress.com

Made in the USA
Lexington, KY
11 December 2011